# Jeremiah Ellison's Poems & Short Stories Collection 2

Most Stories and Poems written by Jeremiah Ellison

"Identity Crisis" written by Matthew Ellison

"A Former Superhero" written by Jeremiah and Matthew Ellison

"Brain-Washing Vaccine" edited by Riley Colins

Cover Art made by Matthew Ellison

Sword Design by Riley Colins

# Content Warning

The following stories contain depictions of racism, mild gore, and political cynicism. The depictions of racism present throughout the book are to showcase the consequences of racism and not to support it in any way possible. The stories will also deal with light commentary on the flaws of the American legal system and is not meant to be harmful or offensive to any particular people/party. Any political commentary is only present to encourage critical thinking of the content. Reader discretion advised.

# Table of Contents

# Poems

# Checklist

Supposedly, life is simple.

Go to school.

Get good grades.

Get a job.

Get Married.

Have kids.

What a load of nonsense.


Go to school.

Easy enough.

Get good grades.

I'm practically a genius.


Get a job.

Let's talk about the pain and triviality of applying in this day and age.

Get married.

Let's talk to the virgins on this topic.

Have kids.

Again, talk to the virgins.


Life is simple, NOT!

Life is difficult,

full of twists and turns.

People don't understand that.

They say they do,

but they really don't.


Fail to do something?

People question your worth.

Don't have a job?

Get back to applying.

Not married?

You just haven't met the right person yet.


What if you already applied to a thousand jobs?

What if you're just shy and get nervous looking at those listings?

What if the right person never comes?

What if they're dead?


Life is not simple,

it is hard.

People don't care about your situation,

they just want to know what you do.


Life is a checklist,

a series of checkmarks,

and missing your checkmarks

is like not existing at all.

# How to Write

Grab a pencil,

a piece of paper

and go to town.

Forget where you are,

immerse yourself in the world.

Go with the flow.


What have you written?

Art, that's what!

But you're not done yet.

Never assume people can read your writing.

Go with the flow.


Grab that computer,

that keyboard,

that whatever

and open up a text editor

be it Word, Google, or other.

Go with the flow.


Type on that keyboard.

Type and type.

Don't be afraid to rewrite that scene.

Never fear rewrites!

Each revision a step closer to your goal!

Go with the flow.


Oh, you're done?

Did you proofread it?

Edit it?

Are you satisfied with it?

Good.

Congratulations!

You wrote a book.

# Praise and Criticism

The pen etches history.

The history I present, everyone loved it.

I spur on,

I write and write,

The praise continues.

Nothing changing

until the praise is broken.

Criticism, meant to improve.

I take my keyboard

and rework my canon.

# Price of a Game

Graduation.

$100.

Groceries.

$70.

Parts for something I don't remember.

$35.

More groceries.

$0.

Birthday.

$50.

3DS parts.

$35.

Misc.

$0.

Holiday.

$50.

That game I've been trying to get this whole time.

$0.

# Late to Work

On my way to work,

and I got a ticket.


No time to waste,

my pay is on the line.


This copper is taking his time.

I ought to put the pedal to the medal.


Instead, I wait

because money is worthless in the joint.


He finally gave it to me,

about damn time.


I speed away,

not flooring it because of that cop.


Let me out of here,

I got a job to do.


I'm late for work,

but that cop is on my hit list.

I am the city accountant,

I determine his paycheck.

# That Dang Video Buffering

I was sitting down on my chair

waiting for my video to load.

As I was sitting down on my chair

waiting for my video to load,

The screen stuttered like a flare

as the progress bar slowed.


That dang video buffering!

That dang video buffering!

Circling around just to make me suffer!


That dang video buffering.

I just wanted to watch an episode.

That dang video buffering!

Can I just watch my episode?

Do you really think you're all that tough?

I'm getting ready to implode.


I've been sitting here for hours.

I've been sitting here for hours.

I could have used this time to develop my brainpower.


Instead, I sit here,

As you buffer.

Instead, I sit here.

As you buffer.

My time is better spent elsewhere.

Consider this connection snuffed.

# Reflection

Across the desolate desert,

a traveler walks.

Wind blowing in utter silence.

He looks down at his blade

that has spilled so much blood.

He marches on, never looking back.


A noise is heard from behind the traveler's back.

The traveler sees another man across the desert.

His face, a mirror reflection soaked in blood.

The traveler ceases walking

as he unsteadily raises his blade

staring in utter silence.


The reflection stares at his foe in deafening silence.

His eyes, daggers being shot back

at the traveler. He raises his own blade

ready to clash across the desert

ending the silence

and refreshing the blade's blood.


The traveler splits open his foe in a splatter of blood.

Over in an instant, all is silent.

He turns around, and walks,

but the deafening static comes back

tenfold. Everything goes fuzzy, thoughts deserting

him as he is pierced by a blade.


The reflection, put back

together, lodged his blade

deep within. Spilling the traveler's blood

over the desert.

An eerie silence

fills the air as the reflection draws back his blade and walks.


He doesn't walk

long. On his side, his blade

He turns back,

dripping from his blade, fresh blood.

The traveler with fuzzy vision stares in silence

as the desert


is stained. The traveler's blood leaks out as his foe stands in silence.

"Who are you?" The foe puts his blade in its sheathe and replies back,

"I am you." He walks into the desert.

# **The Passage of Time** *after Shakespeare Sonnet 19 by William Shakespeare*

Time, a river flowing ever ceaselessly.

Waiting to drown you in the dark abyss.

Hang on for dear life as you make your peace,

for time will not wait for your dismissal.

Yet, let time continue its long crossing

as we sail across its long, endless stream.

Stretching across, all over the world, tossing.

However, there is one thing it shall not reap.

Our meaning on this overly harsh, cruel world.

No matter what history scribes,

our presence is felt as our life unfurls,

no matter how history chooses to describe.

     Do your worst Time, as I stand my ground here!

     I will not move, nor will I disappear.

# **Relic Forest** *After the song from Pokémon Colosseum/Pokémon XD Gale of Darkness*[1]

At the end of a dark tunnel,

lies a peaceful forest.

A stone pathway with a shrine at the end.

Its protector gives the forest

a healing power.

To dissolve the shadows,

created by man,

and allow light and warmth

back into their heart.

A place nearly untouched by man,

Where nature roams free.

Dispel the shadows.

----

[1] This poem is only inspired by the song of the same name and is not officially associated with the Pokémon franchise. Please support the official release.

# **I'm Always Running** *after the song by AJ Dispirito*[2]

Eyes shrouded in the darkest glow.

I think I can see it show.

Your eyes contain a spark, you know.

Open up your eyes and see me go.


The past, lost and gone, forgotten.

All the life we've ever been through.

Remind me on what has fallen

As the cold air always blows blue.


This world never knew my game.

I hope I have a chance to stay.

Floating on my own with no shame.

These arms, are worn, never fading.


I keep moving, never stopping.
I'm always running!

---

[2] This poem is only inspired by the song of the same name and is not associated with Meta Runner in any official capacity. Here's a link to the official video: https://www.youtube.com/watch?v=-XkT5JVVlmI. Please support the official release.

# Burning City

Endless fiery flames burning

as bright as a thousand suns

stretching as far as the eye can see.

Once proud buildings, swept in the raging inferno

Creating a landscape known as hell.

Darkness no longer creeps

in this land that was once my home.

I run away from the madness

as explosions sound off in the distance.

Buildings fall shaking the very Earth.

I fall down onto the jagged street.

All my bones crying in agony.

As the flames roar, all around me.

The sound of helicopter blades close in.

Echoed by the laughter of a madman.

I burst into tears as he climbs down

and grabs me

and takes me to parts unknown.

# Burning City (Original)

Endless fiery flames burning

as bright as a thousand suns

stretching as far as the eye can see.

Once proud buildings now ablaze,

in shambles because of the flames.

Darkness no longer creeps

in the endless sea of flames.

The ground broken into pieces

as gravel plunges into the abyss.

Buildings fall in the distance,

Never to be seen again.

A person stands on the other side in the inferno,

flames erupt from his flesh

burning them down to a crisp.

Cracks form in the ground

breaking apart plunging me into the abyss.

# Winter Wonderland

I'd like to go to Paris in the Spring.

But, the city is coated in permanent frost.

With you, I'm up for almost anything.


The Eifel Tower, tall and proud like a king.

Its splendor never lost.

I'd like to go to Paris in the spring.


Snow has turned Paris into a winter wonderland.

As if a spell was cast.

With you, I'm up for almost anything.


Sparkling ice coating the street.

Frozen statues of all who were lost.

I'd like to go to Paris in the Spring.


Many statues lost, as the cold sings

a song of one who is crossed.

But with you, I'm up for almost anything.


The land barren with empty swings,

A land never to defrost.

I'd like to...go to Paris...in the Spring.

With you…I'm up…for almost anything.


*Shatter*

# Short Stories

29

# A Statue And Its Cat Redux

*<The following story was originally written for Twitter and its original format will be closely preserved.>*

It's another dark and stormy night, folks. Keep an eye out for any statues coming to life this night, and if you see any, please report them to the Statue Housing Agency and kindly direct them to the nearest SHA facility. This is an official announcement from the SHA.

A statue has been reported coming to life at the corner of Washington and Lincoln Ave. Eyewitness reports claim that the statue has picked up a cat and is currently taking it to a veterinarian.

As a reminder to everyone under the Statue Animation Act, upon a statue's initial animation all expenses before being housed are covered by the SHA in order to help the animated statue integrate into society easier.

The statue has been reported to be at the Veterinarians office having the cat he previously picked up get a checkup. A relatively common occurrence upon initial animation since many animals like to hide in nearby bushes and hedges near the statues.

The rain is now subsiding and the statue has been properly redirected to an SHA facility. According to an eyewitness report, the statue was spotted heading over towards the nearest SHA facility where it will be housed and properly integrated into society.

For those of you unfamiliar with the job market, animated statues are highly sought after for physical labor especially in the transport of large and heavy objects as they are not bound by the laws of human limitation.

Some companies actually prefer employing statues as opposed to buying and operating heavy machinery as it reduces the expenses of teaching the operation of said machinery to new employees along with reducing the need for maintenance cost of said machinery.

The statue has successfully arrived at a SHA facility and is now in the process of being integrated with society. It is a long and tedious process that involves steps including registering yourself for citizenship, getting an ID, etc.

We of the Statue Housing Agency would like to thank everyone today for your cooperation in guiding this newly animated statue towards us. He will be housed in a few days and will be available for employment afterwards.

If you are interested in employing this statue, please contact us at 1-800-555-SHAE.

Have a nice day everyone and let's continue to help all the statues integrate into society.

# Twitter's Server[3]

*<The following story was originally written for Twitter and its original format will be closely preserved.>*

**Now connecting to Twitter.com.**

**Connecting**

**Connecting**

**Connection established. Now inputting credentials.**

**Log in successful. Now testing tweeting capability.**

**Error! Connection attempts accidentally tweeted.**

**Assessing situation.**

**Result: Accidental tweets are harmless.**

**Now activating scanner.**

**Scanning subject Pokemiah.**

**Scanning**

**Scanning**

**Scan complete.**

**Virtualization!**

Ok, computer. I have landed inside the server.

Wait, did it just tweet that?

**Affirmative. Speech translates directly to text within the server.**

---

Seriously? Must be a logic error in the code. Oh well. Not much I can do about it.

I do admit, while I wasn't expecting any actual sort of environment, it's weird seeing all these tweets just floating around.

And it's a bit dis-jarring to see a tweet appear right next to me every time I make a comment.

***Analysis**: Complaining will get you no where in life*.

Why did I program you with sass?

***Answer**: You wanted me to have a charming personality*.

*sigh* Whatever. Let's just get to our mission. Where's the virus?

*Searching*

***Virus located**. **Current Location**: **Business Sector***.

Alright then. Computer, activate narration mode.

***Why do I have a narration mode***?

Because it's cool.

***Error**! Failure to understand user logic*.

*Now activating narration mode*.

Finally.

*Subject Pokemiah proceeds to run across the barren landscape representative of the Twitter server in cyberspace*.

*Various tweets floating in the air in every facet of the digital sky*.

*No skybox exists. The floor is just a digital construct full of black tiles with green outlines*.

*Subject Pokemiah proceeds to double-check virus location using the map prompt above his arm simultaneously running towards the designated location.*

*Virus successfully located by subject.*

*Virus's Current Form: A gigantic, green, digital centipede.*

*It crunches on a tweet floating in the air, presumably about the stock market, as subject Pokemiah preps deletion program.*

*Deletion program form, requested by subject: Lasersword, reminiscent of Lightsabers from Star Wars.*

*Subject proceeds to engage virus program, running straight at it. Virus fails to notice subject.*

*Subject successfully cuts virus into two near base. Virus deletion: 20%.*

*Virus is now roaring in anger at the loss of two layers of legs and proceeds to chase after subject.*

Looks like big, fat, and ugly knows I'm here. Good. Let's give it the old one-two.

*Subject turns back and runs back at the virus, sword ready to slash it in half.*

*Virus shows signs of intelligence and proceeds to burrow underneath data structure designated as floor.*

*Subject continues to run towards the hole and foolishly jumps into it before peering down the hole.*

*Result: Subject is now in free-fall as no floor exists underneath.*

Can you please help me here, Computer!? Preferably before I fall into the Deep Web.

*Now launching hover-board.exe*.

Ok, there is no way you can tell me that the pony textures are randomly generated and what's with the ice cream truck music?

**You never asked me for any specific textures for the hover-board and I thought you would like some spice for your boss fight**.

Funny. Real funny.

**Subject proceeds to mount hover-board and flies back up to the virus currently floating in mid-air**.

**Virus resurfaces before subject can reach it**.

I don't know how you were floating in mid-air, nor do I care. Computer, give me my gun!

**You do not have any programs resembling that of a gun**.

Gosh dang it, computer!

**Subject continues pursuit of virus speeding up on his hoverboard, safely above ground**.

**The virus suddenly turns around and attempts to devour the subject**.

**Error**!

**Error**!

**Virus has devoured subject and**

*!elona em evaeL*

**Virus is currently leaving business sector and heading toward Anime sector**.

**Subject has been lost**

**Chances of recovery**: 10%.

*Preparing for worst case scenario*.

*Observation: Deletion program is now protruding from stomach of virus*.

*Virus is sliced in half and promptly deleted*.

Who told you we could have a fake-out death here because I sure didn't! Computer disengage factory reset.

*Affirmative*.

Well, that takes cares of the virus, unless there's any others I should know about.

*Negative*.

In that case, beam me up Scotty!

*Did you want me to cross off "Watch Star Trek" on your to-do list*?

No, not yet.

*Affirmative. Now prepping rematerialization protocol*.

*Extracting user data*.

*Extraction complete. Devirtualization in progress*.

*Devirtualizing*

*Devirtualizing*

*Devirtualization complete*.

*Checking Materialization*.

*Complete. No errors detected*.

*Now logging out*.

# <u>COVID-19 Saga</u>

## Past: A World Filled With Fear

Spring break is over, the calm should end as we go back to the daily grind of school life and continue our learning experiences in a calm, orderly fashion. That's how it's supposed to go but in this experience we call life nothing ever goes as planned. The worldwide pandemic known as either the Coronavirus or COVID-19 hit the nation like a typhoon rocking it to its very core not physically but spiritually. This pandemic has sent everyone into a panic cleaning out store shelves as if it's going out of style. Wal-marts as barren as a desert, something I never thought I would see. There is no rhyme nor reason to their action, just a catalyst. And here I am, in the blast zone.

At first, this thing didn't concern me in the least bit as I can be pretty apathetic to the craziness of the world. Plus, throughout my life surfing on the Internet I often question everything I see on it unless I'm purposefully searching for it. The information I chose to believe was that this was indeed a new strand of a pre-existing virus and that the survivability rate was quite high. While it has gotten worse like any disease the real problem is fear. This fear has sent everyone into hiding for fear that they may catch the virus. It began affecting me when Spring Break was suddenly extended. That was the calm before the storm as the chaos ensued. Slowly, everything under the sun began to shut down one after the other and you could very well see the chaos behind the scenes. The emails sent to me by the instructors along with the campus announcements were evidence enough of that chaos as they were scrambling behind the scenes to move everything from the material plain into cyberspace.

The move into cyberspace is quite jarring and taxing. The uncertainty of everything, the decompressed lesson times, and most importantly the sheer amount of homework. It feels like the semester is almost at its end as the big assignments approach their due date. On top of that, I have to manually keep up with all the lecture material taking up a lot more time that it used to. The sheer volume of it exponentially increasing as the stress of it all enters my brain and overloads it forcing me to reboot. This isn't the first time I dealt with online classes as I taken a couple during my last years in RLC to finish up my degree, but I didn't like them that much. I honestly don't think that online lessons stick with me as well as in person lectures but in a world consumed with fear, we must all adapt.

# Future: The Future

COVID19 has ended and all is right in the world. At least, that's what I want to say but life isn't that simple. The COVID19 pandemic of 2020 was a very stressful time for everyone and revealed a lot of flaws with our current economic infrastructure and technology. Alas, one of the things many people were most ill-prepared for was the move of almost everything into cyberspace. Many people were scared of even being at **risk** of infection causing many small businesses to shut down and plenty of people adjusting to their new life of working at home. Now that COVID19 has ended, companies are taking great strides to make sure something like this doesn't happen again. They're currently reviewing all their equipment and software that they use for manufacturing and production of goods and entertainment to analyze what can be reasonably done from home and how best to implement it. Of course, many companies are also using it as an excuse to try and abolish sick days, but they haven't told anyone about that agenda yet. While this is the route some of them have chosen, others are going more so towards the route of automation and cutting out the middle man. Their logic: "You can't get sick if you're a machine." Which yes is true, but it'll leave many people out of a job and inflation has been steadily raising prices ever since the minimum wage increased. That is also another reason companies are going this route: human labor costs. Unfortunately, due to this increase in minimum wage, companies in their infinite greed are trying to minimize their labor costs by taking out the human element and instead replacing us with machines like self-checkout, automated production machines, etc. If they think it will reduce their expenses in the future, they'll do it.

Schools were also hit pretty hard, if not the hardest, by the 2020 pandemic as everyone was rushing to move all their schoolwork and assignments to a digital format and many teachers were ill-trained for the job leading to an excess of homework for the students and a loss of interaction for many teachers. By the second semester, teachers got smarter and started using Zoom to communicate with their students and learned how best to give a moderate amount of homework without overwhelming the student. People are now returning to in-person lectures and some people are thriving now as they just couldn't handle online classes. It's very stressful. However, the schools learned from their errors and are devising better ways students can work from home along with making training for instruction of online classes mandatory for the teachers, along with a mandatory class for students that just teaches them how to participate in an online class, but that one I believe is only a half-semester class.

In addition, schools are looking into alternate ways of instructing classes online since Zoom is not infallible. Some companies are looking to capitalize on the market by making highly questionable programs. What I mean by highly questionable is in terms of privacy as some of these programs kind of resemble malware with the permissions they give the school and provider such as the ability to turn on other people's cameras, look at a student's screen without permission, etc. Highly shady if you ask me.

Another avenue they're looking at is using the popular game VR Chat, which to contrary belief does not require a VR headset to play, to teach class as you could have virtual classrooms that could work as substitutes for the real thing until you remember that your teacher is using a Joker avatar. And I mean the one from Batman, not Persona. And then, you got that one classmate with a loli avatar using a voice filter to make him sound like one and the teacher has no clue why. Then, the next class day everyone else comes to class with an FBI agent avatar except the one guy who didn't get the joke along with the teacher. That was an interesting Wednesday.

You think with how important the internet has become thanks to the pandemic that they would just give away hi-speed internet for free at this point. But once again, humans are greedy creatures and will never give away anything like that for free if they can so help it. I mean I understand not having free internet using fiber optic cables as those are dangerous to maintain and I don't think a government worker's salary is worth the risk, unless it pays like Congress. Of course, this is just me assuming and I could be wrong.

Speaking of politics, Trump was **not** reelected[4] as many people were not satisfied about how he handled the pandemic, or his conduct in general, and the icing on the cake was when he got the coronavirus himself and completely disregards everything he told other people to do. Ironic, isn't it? He survived, but Biden became the president because most people don't seem to believe in third parties and many people are questioning his agendas, but that comes with the territory of being president. As long as he doesn't do something stupid as try to take away our guns or start a nuclear war, I think we'll be fine but I don't like talking about politics in general so there's that. This Nancy Pelosi person also got arrested for destroying classified documents that many believe would have been her downfall. Now people are having a hard time finding evidence to support this claim, but I wouldn't be surprised to find out that it's true.

Because of the stress the whole pandemic had on the economy and the country in general, both the president and Congress are working together with the World Health Organization and plenty of misc. epidemic experts on how best to tackle a repeat of this exact scenario going so far as to draft a bill with a plan in place in case this ever happens again. Many people are unsure of this bill. Others are watching it closely to see if it's better than Trump's plan. And there are some who think that it's a great idea. While the consensus varies, all agree that the government needs one if it ever happens again.

By the way, we found out where the Murder Hornets disappeared to. They ended up somewhere near the coastline of California.[5] The government is already taking measures to ensure that they aren't too big of a problem, but I think the alligators got it handled. Now if only everything was going this smoothly.

---

[4] This was written during 2020 when Trump was still president.
[5] This may be inaccurate as it was written in 2020 before they were rediscovered on the North American continent. This section of the COVID-19 Saga is fictional therefore not everything is going to be accurate and is just one interpretation of a possible future.

"Earlier today, another young man by the name of Ariadne Pablo was murdered by a police officer while he was on patrol. Pablo was accused of shoplifting at a nearby store and according to the police officer who killed him…"

From stories I read online, he didn't actually shoplift from that store. Quite the opposite actually, he left a donation there as the store is a small and super friendly local business that just barely survived the Coronavirus and has helped numerous people in their time of need. It's quite saddening to hear he died shortly after. Hey, the shopkeeper is on the news.

"Ariadne was always a kind young man. I've known him since he was a small child."

Unfortunately, this isn't the first case of police brutality. Quite recently, the trials involving the murder of several black folk have ended with none of the murderers convicted. This isn't simply a problem of police brutality but racism in general. The Black Lives Matter movement is at an all time high after these trials ended staging peaceful protests, some of which devolve into tear gas and riots. However, a few of them have joined into a new group called the Black Lives Coalition. An explosion?

I look behind me and see a building collapsing. I quickly run out of there before the building can land on me barely avoiding it. This was not a controlled explosion by a construction company. It's the latest assault by the Black Lives Coalition. A group of extremists who are tired of oppression and have decided that the best way to incite change is to murder innocent civilians. The building they just blew up belonged to a company that recently laid off a ton of workers, most of which were black. Now they have every right to be angry about everything that has happened to them, but murdering unrelated people is cruel. Crap, I see them. They have guns ready to kill off stragglers. I need to get out of here fast. With groceries in hand, I run. I run far away from the scene dialing 911 as I was running, informing them of what's going on. It doesn't take long for them to arrive on the scene. I learned later that they were able to arrest several members of the Coalition who then drank liquid cyanide to commit suicide afterwards. Unfortunately, this will not stop until people put aside their racism and prejudice in order to reform the system in a positive light. Only then can we prevent another 2000 deaths.

Life is hard. The future is not always bright, but if you keep an open mind, you can get through the bad and find the good.

*<COVID-19 Saga End>*

# The Second American Civil War

Fires everywhere, gunshots in the background. Everything has gone to shit. No matter where you look, everything is just a remnant of its former self. How did we get here? What went wrong? How am I still alive? I want to say it started in 2020, but that would be wrong. That was just where it became its most prominent. Well, it used to be anyway.

During these past 5 years, police brutality has skyrocketed and guess who the primary victims are. That's right, black folks. I have no qualms against them. They're human just like the rest of us and deserve human rights just like the rest of us, but…

An explosion just went off in the background because another black man threw a grenade at a group of police officers. I wish this was the only thing wrong with the world but if we look over there, we can see another problem. Behind this building lies an ongoing feminist rally. When this second civil war started, it wasn't just black people against the police and white people. Women, tired of being underpaid and underappreciated with many men degrading them combined with various cases of rapists getting minimal penalties, decided to take a stand for themselves at the beginning of this war. Some of them take a more peaceful approach to addressing these issues. And there's a tear gas canister landing in the middle of it. And where did she get that machine gun?

I run from the building before more blood is shed. While those are two factions, they're not the only ones. There are several smaller factions, like various minority groups and economic classes, going to war against each other. When one thing exploded out of proportion, everything else collapsed and here we find ourselves in this hellscape we call America. Every injustice, every wrong, everything wrong with the country exploded all at once sparking the second American Civil War.

These injustices are real, but at this point there's not a country left. Just an inferno of fire and violence. It doesn't help that the president locked himself up in the White House. I'm one of the people who didn't join a faction. Heck, I'm just trying to get some exercise. People believe the apocalypse would be caused by nukes, but no. Humans are the real monsters. Humanity as a whole is a violent species, hardcoded into our DNA. We unite against what we perceive as singular extraordinarily evil entities. But what happens if there is not a singular entity to blame but a vast majority of people to blame? This. This is what happens.

Buildings are on fire, car alarms and police sirens in the background. Various bloody battles everywhere. It's a mad house I tell you. A mad house! I keep walking trying to get back to what is as close to home as I can get. Alas, on my way there I run into Black folks. Like I said, no disrespect towards them, but I'm White so therefore on their hitlist.

The big guy with a grenade in his hand asks, "Where do you think you're going?"

"Nowhere. Just…home. I guess," I answer downtrodden.

"Well then. Tell me, why should I let you go home? Do you know how many of us were killed while you Whites walk away? Give me a reason why I shouldn't off you right now," says the defacto leader.

"I never supported those who murdered you guys in cold blood. Look, everything has gone to shit. Just let me pass and I won't harm any of you."

The guy steps aside and I walk. All their guns aimed at me. This is normal. Nobody trusts anybody outside their own faction. In case you're wondering, I am armed. Nobody in their right mind would go out unarmed nowadays. I'm still looking for a bulletproof vest in order to further protect myself, but those are so scare due to demand that I don't even know where to get one. Money is practically obsolete these days and everyone loots one another to survive. I walk past them all and they walk away. These were some of the more reasonable people. If I was in a big group, I would be shot or blown up. In the end, there's nothing left of America. No glory, no law, just anarchy. I arrive back home which is just a multi-level mall parking lot. These structures are quite sturdy and it does the job but man do I miss the good old days where the only thing I had to worry about was what I could afford rather than where can I find something remotely edible. I sometimes had to resort to eating rats for dinner. That's how bad it is. I sit back and get ready for another ratburger.

# Brain-Washing Vaccine

I was walking down the street staring down at my phone when I look up, and out of the corner of my eye I spot my friend's back. Once I saw him, I immediately put my phone in my pocket and walked up to him.

"Hey, wanna hang out later?"

"…"

"Hello?..."

When I turn him around, not knowing what to expect, I see his blank expression with his glossy eyes. The color could not be perceived in his irises. Only the whites of his eyes. No emotion, no desire, no free will. Just nothing. "What happened to you, bro?"

"…Vac…cine."

Vaccine? What vaccine could he be talking…about? I look in the direction of a billboard advertising the overly rushed vaccine for DIVOC-91. That's when it hit me. Just last year, a new disease called DIVOC-91 appeared out of nowhere killing a great amount of people. It killed about half of China's population before spreading to the other parts of the world. While the death toll in the various other countries were less than what they had been in China, they were still pretty significant in comparison, such as 15% of the US population, 30% of India, etc. Now being a year later, they developed a vaccine for the disease, but I never got vaccinated myself. Not because I don't trust vaccines, but because I don't trust in this specific one. I did some research online, but there's so little data about it that I can't make an informed decision. Not to mention I don't like needles. I practically get a panic attack every time I see one. In other words, I'm not sure even if I did choose to get it if I would have the ability to stay still long enough to be injected. There's also no available data on the long-term side-effects due to how quickly it was rushed out the door. Still, lately, something's been off. Snapping back to the present, the shell of my friend walks back into the crowd, like a mindless zombie congregating into a horde filled to the brim with other mindless zombies.

From that point onward, I couldn't get a hold of any of my other friends. When I do see them, they work like machines with no breaks. Never speaking. And it's not just limited to my friends. Everyone is affected. No one complains. No one talks. No one plays. Even the children. All they seem to do is just go to school and come back home. In fact, I don't even see them with friends. All I see are those glossy, soulless eyes.

In the distance, I hear construction work going on, but nobody is talking. There is drool hanging from their mouths, as if in a trance. I walk down the street to my market research firm. Lately, there has been a sharp decline in the entertainment industry. Movies, books, games, they're all selling less than before, and it keeps exponentially decreasing as if people don't care anymore about entertainment. Even the adult films have dropped sales.

I see a couple of people I know, Dave and Goliath, who work in the medical field. I know them through work as they've help me collect data on the sales of medical supplies and equipment. We usually chat over a piping hot cup of coffee at the local café near both my firm and the hospital. Even though we primarily meet for business, we often chat about our lives and how our days at work are going. Oh, the horror stories they've told me, and what's even worse, they can just laugh it off. Are all doctors like this? Sometimes, I take quick sips of my coffee to hide my nervousness. Thank goodness these guys didn't major in psychology. I walk up to them in order to ask them the question that's been haunting my mind as of lately.

"Hey, have you noticed how weird people have been acting?"

They glance at each other nervously, sweating bullets. Then when Dave and Goliath looked around they noticed blank eyes staring in their direction. Some of the eyes coming to a complete standstill. Just looking at us, the drooling masses with their soulless eyes staring daggers at us. It sent a shiver down all of our spines.

And out of nowhere, they bend down to my ear whispering, "It's not safe to talk here."

They usher me into a dark alley. Now normally I wouldn't even consider going into such an unsafe place especially with the looming threat of a possible mugging, but I know these guys. So naturally, I trust them. We walk into the dark alley completely shrouded in shadows. There was a dumpster next to the wall, and next to it a pile of trash with a fly annoyingly buzzing its wings. A far cry from the bristling metropolis that seems to be more reminiscent of a mental asylum as of late with the way people have been moving and acting. They bend down to my ears and one whispers, "Whatever you do, don't get the vaccine."

"We examined it ourselves and found something…horrifying," states the other.

The sheer fact that they find it horrifying is triggering all kinds of red flags in my brain. What can be so bad that it can scare doctors?

They continue, "A little microscopic device. Upon discovery, we immediately took it to that inventor/tinkerer down the road asking for his input."

"Between the three of us, we noticed that it attaches itself to dendrites and sends false neuron signals to the brain overriding basic cognitive function."

"It erases desire, wants, personality. It's essentially brainwashing."

Now that is horrifying. But there's no way that could be real, right? Plus, there seems to be one flaw in their argument, "But didn't you guys get the vaccine? After all, aren't medical professionals required to get it?"

They look at each other once more and see someone gazing at us through the alley. One rushes and grabs him, dragging them into the alley. They hold him down to the ground and inject him with something. Then, he just stops moving. Did they just…kill him?

The one holding the syringe, Dave, continues, "That was a close one. And to answer your question, no. That was a lie. What the government told the public. At least partially."

Goliath continues, "They gave us a different vaccine. But…that one contains…"

He was shaking in fear, unable to speak.

Dave finishes, "A bomb. If they catch the slightest wind of what we told you, they will detonate all the cells in our body and kill us in cold blood. That's why we had to kill him."

Goliath mutters, "The z…z…patients, yeah, patients, are programmed to…"

He stops. Dave finishes walking up to me, "They are programmed to look for those that the government would define as troublesome and report to them."

He places his hand on my shoulder and finishes, "Just be careful. One wrong move, and you'll be the government's idea of a perfect human being."

They walked away. I couldn't believe it. Mind control? That sounds so unbelievably far-fetched. Yet, I don't have a better explanation for it. Plus, they killed a man, in cold blood. There is no way any of this is real, right?

A few weeks later, they finally passed those gun control laws they were trying to pass for the past couple of years, and nobody was arguing about it except a vocal minority on Twitter who never got vaccinated. Even then, some of these spiels sounded like the work of conspiracy nuts. There were a few, more telligible, replies thankfully. That was the second red flag I saw proving this mind control. It gradually got worse and worse. The next thing they did was require every citizen to get vaccinated and all "anti-vaxxers" as they called it were to be forcibly vaccinated and thrown into prison. I've seen many people get dragged off by these "zombies" to who knows where. I managed to save a few, but that required…well…sacrificing…my conscious? no, my peace of mind. They started imposing curfews as a way to both direct the zombies back home to sleep and to track the "anti-vaxxers". Gosh, why did they have to use that term here? I mean come on! Couldn't they have given us a better name than reusing that horrible derogatory term for people who just don't plain believe in vaccines.

Thankfully, they never came to my door. Of course, I've increased all the locks on it. They also upped the taxes because of greed. With everyone brainwashed or fearing for their lives, nobody is going to publicly argue with you about it. The lack of basic cognition and companies' focus on maximizing profits left many citizens to starve, fall ill, and wallow in their own filth. Public health has become a joke. Many children were unable to eat, and some even went homeless once more due to the parent/caretakers' inability to care for them anyway thanks to insufficient funds and no mental capability to look after them. I'm pretty sure reproduction was only allowed because we need to survive as a species. Most of this was happening either at orphanages and/or foster homes where they didn't care about the children enough to even consider vaccinating them.

However, some people out in the country actually managed to avoid the vaccinations altogether and gosh darn it, the hillbillies are the safest people to be around now. Especially since they still have their guns. A couple of times, I actually stayed over at a nearby hillbilly house when I feared for my own safety. The internet was slowly being censored. You couldn't use curse words, say anything bad about the government, and if you violate any rules, the police will knock down your door shortly afterwards. After seeing it happen firsthand at my neighbor's house, I put my phone in airplane mode, filled my bathtub with water, and dropped it in effectively frying it. At this point, I couldn't take it. I packed up my things, hopped into my car, and left for Canada. At this point, there is no saving this country. On my way there, I threw my phone out the window and into a creek. I'm taking out the middleman so they can't track me. And that is how I moved to Canada.

Five years later, and I'm living a comfortable life in Canada. I got a decent job. I cut wood and sell it. I live in a log cabin in a snowy region close to Alaska so it's in high demand. However, the situation with the U.S. has gotten even worse in these past five years. I make it a point to keep tabs on the whole political conflict the U.S. has internationally and gather up what news I can on the old home front. The previous president was assassinated, presumably by poison. So the job went to his vice president who was also killed giving it to the speaker of the house, Chancy Nolowski. One of her first orders of business was to remove the presidential term limit set in place after Roosevelt's terms, presumably so she could remain in control indefinitely. Ever since then, the other nations have caught wind of the brain-washing technology employed by the U.S. on its citizens. Due to the appalling lack of free will the technology provides its citizens, they were ousted from the United Nations and are not to be reinstated until they remove the effects of the brain-washing vaccine. Surprising no one, they didn't. Instead, they teamed up with the nations in **favor** of the vaccine and essentially created the Neo Axis Powers. Clearly, they were inspired by World War II. A knock can be heard at my door.

"Come in."

The door opens revealing a young man dressed in a thick parka with a wool cap over his head and determined black eyes, "Are you ready for the meeting?"

"Bring them in."

He nods and closes the door. A minute later, a myriad of men and women, all refugees from the U.S. just like me gather in my cabin. It is time to begin the meeting. A woman with orange hair tied in a bun slams a circular container on the wooden table and opens it revealing test tubes with a red liquid inside. "This is the antidote to the vaccine invented by the U.S. We should have enough in supply to poison the water supply of a small town in Alaska. However, we still need test subjects, as this antidote is largely untested."

I state, "So the mission today is rather simple. Rendezvous at the breach with our guide and capture test subjects who have been vaccinated with this brain washing technology. We need to know how effective it is."

Everyone nods and we stand up and get onto our buggies. We drive to the breach and see our contact from the Alaskan mafia. Turns out, crime isn't a very profitable business if you can't find anyone willing to commit it. They guide us to the boss's chambers and he's a big fat man smoking a cigar. He gives us the go-ahead and even provides us with two men highly skilled in kidnapping. It's very sad that the world needs people experienced in that field right now. We drive into the breach onto Alaskan soil and stop dead near a town. We are then transferred to a black van and drive into town. Luckily, many people still have their cars from before they were brainwashed, so we don't stick out as much as we could have. We go to a far-off corner of the street and park. While we would like to do it in a more remote place, the brain-washing makes our targets unlikely to go to bars, so here we are. Somebody walks by, and we quickly open the doors and grab him covering his mouth as he tries to scream. We gag him and tie him up. For the initial testing, we want at least 4 to 5 subjects. We were able to grab three before having to leave because people were starting to get suspicious. However, on the way back, the kidnappers managed to grab a fourth one that we were about to pass by, stuffing him into a sack and tossing him in the floor. Am I glad I was never a target of theirs. We made it back to the breach and took the subjects into a tent.

From there, Dr. Honeybun opened the container and put the liquid into a syringe. She injected it into Subject 1 and he screams in pain, starts gasping for breath, and nearly choking spits something out. It was swept up and quickly placed into a jar, as much as we could get anyway. Dr. Honeybun places a dropper in there and sucks it up and places it on a microscope slide. It takes a few attempts until she finds what she's looking for: the nanobot, or nanomachine, causing this. The guy groans and asks, "Where am I?" He notices he's tied up and starts screaming and panicking.

"Who are you people? Where am I? What have you done with my wife and kids? What are you going to do with me? What are you-"

Dr. Honeybun looks at him with her glasses shrouded in malice. This never ends well. She kicks the man knocking him down to the floor. She says, "You're lucky to have your free will back. We do not know where your wife and kids are at. All we know is that you have been a literal zombie since you got vaccinated. Now shut up and quit your whining or I'll shove my foot so far up your-"

"*Ahem*"

She bites her tongue making a partial hissing noise. She walks off as I set the chair upright and untie him. "Sorry about that, she is easily agitated."

"Yeah, my wife had quite a temper too."

I state calmly, "She's not my wife. She's just the head researcher of the Resistance, Dr. Honeybun. Simply put, you've been in a trance-like state for the past 5 years or so, and are now just coming out of it. You probably have several questions, but this is not the time nor the place."

Dr. Honeybun preps another sample as he looks and stops at the vacant stares of the other subjects. "How long?"

"Hmm?"

Dr. Honeybun walks over to the next subject. "How long was I…like that?"

She injects the antidote into the second subject who starts screaming in agony.

I bite my lips and answered, "As I stated previously, five years."

The next subject coughs something up, presumably his machine. It is swept and put into a jar. He asks, "Where can I go for answers?"

I beckon him and say, "Follow me, if you want to live."

# The Butterfly Effect

## Part 1: The Revolutionary War

*<Disclaimer: These next three stories are supposed to be an alternate timeline where history went differently and is not meant to be historically accurate.>*

Back in 1776, General George Washington is having his trusty crew row across a lake in order to ambush the British army. The crewmate right behind him rowing suddenly feels a sudden pressure in his nostrils.

"A…A…Achoo!"

The force of his sneeze sends his head back suddenly hitting the rear of General Washington with enough force to knock him off-balance causing him to fall in the lake. The soldiers look down where he fell as he sank to the bottom, the weight of his musket causing him to sink down further. He tries to swim back up, but inevitably drowns. And that was the story of how General Washington died and failed his soldiers. They were able to just barely succeed in the ambush that day thanks to the many field simulations they done before, but after Washington's death command of the American forces was handed over to John Hancock who proved to be incompetent on the field of the battle. Even with the help of the Native Americans, he proved time and time again that he was not cut out for the field of battle as he kept falling for the enemies' traps and eventually died after reloading his musket the wrong way causing him to shoot his own head off.

John Hancock's lousy leadership in the war allowed the British the perfect opportunity to launch a counterattack on the Americans. John didn't always follow the Native Americans' advice thus making it easier for the British to lure them out into the open. Thanks to some successful captures, they found out the source for the Americans' advantage in the War: the Native Americans. The British then decided to commit total genocide of Native Americans leading to the loss of the greatest asset America had in the Revolutionary War. It took about 10 years to eliminate all the tribes, but they eventually succeeded and apprehended the American Resistance.

Shortly afterwards, the King and Queen of England arrived in America themselves where the Americans launched one last desperate ambush, but they were no match for the royal guard. The king personally took it upon himself to burn the Declaration of Independence in front of the very people who were hoping for the freedom it would provide them in a public demonstration of power. From there, he told all Americans to relinquish their weapons or be horribly executed. As an example, he held a public execution right then and there of everyone who signed the Declaration of Independence along with many major figures of the Revolutionary War.

Defeated and demoralized, America relinquished its weapons and surrendered to the British Empire where it became the British Colonies once more before it was renamed to New England.

# Part 2: World War II

The year is 1942 and the British navy is facing a war like it's never seen before. Htiler has started his assault on the world plunging it in its entirety into World War II. Dissatisfied with the ending of World War I, known back then as the Great War he decided to personally lead Germany on a crusade against all who oppose them making them believe that they are superior to all races. Thus, World War II begun.

Currently, the British Navy is trying to combat the aerial forces of the Luftwaffle bombers. Despite their best efforts, they're no match for the German aircraft as they drop their bombs onto the many ships of the Navy. Meanwhile, Panzer tanks are attacking them from the dock launching myriads of ballista at the ships. Many ships start sinking into the dark, murky depths as the crew scrambles towards the lifeboats. A tank fires another volley launching many people into the water and killing many others. The ships sank and Germany seizes control of England.

The few survivors that were able to escape moved inland in order to warn the king and queen. Upon hearing the news, they were en-raged by the Germans' conduct and sent a myriad of troops to oppose them. In order to strengthen their numbers, they drafted the citizens of New England as soldiers and ordered them to fight in the name of Great Britain. Alas, it did not go as planned. Germany's blitzkrieg strategy was still highly effective against the British army. New England soldiers were more likely to either desert the army or commit suicide. Usually by pointing their gun at their head. However, many have also kept themselves informed of the events of WWII and decided to side with the lesser of two evils becoming some of the best soldiers Great Britain had to offer.

Eventually, the Nazis did make it to the royal palace. However, when they got there the king and queen had already fled to New England. From there they directed their forces and cooperated with the Allied Powers for the D-Day invasion of France. But, their plans were leaked to the enemy. A few of the citizens of New England were fed up with the king and queen's rule and decided to ally with the Axis powers. They infiltrated the British army and used it as a means to find out the plans of the Allied Powers. With that information, the German occupied region of Normandy was further fortified and prepared for the attack. The Allies lost as their armies were decimated, one right after the other. It was a bloody massacre that affected the entirety of the Allied Powers.

There wasn't a single survivor and if there was, they were never found. While the Allies were twiddling their thumbs trying to figure out their next move, Japan decided to deal the finishing blow. It bombed Pearl Harbor in the outer reaches of New England destroying whatever military might they had left. Afterwards, they surrendered and as a gesture of good will relinquished New England to the hands of the Nazis.

# Part 3: War in New England

"Ok, as we all learned throughout history, the Nazi party has been occupying New England ever since 1942 when they blitzkrieged the Navy in Great Britain and destroyed the entirety of the British Naval Forces. They tried offsetting this loss by deploying troops drafted in New England over to Britain, who unfortunately all died during D-Day. When our defenses were weakened, Japan sent in a strike team and bombed Pearl Harbor and after our catastrophic loss there, gave the territory over to the Nazi party as a gesture of good will. Now, it was very clear from the get-go how little the monarchy cared for the residents of New England as they worked us just as bad as slaves leaving most citizens at the brink of exhaustion. Things improved a bit around 1830 when the abolishment of the Slave Trade got the British citizens to question the conditions in New England, but that was just them saving face. That brings us here to the present day. The Nazis are ten times worse than the British monarchy, yet we don't want the monarchy back either. We are here to incite a rebellion, much like General Washington attempted back in 1776 before his untimely demise. The plan is simple, we secure the port town of Waterloo Crescendo. From there, we have to drive the Nazis back into their boats. Once inside, we let them take off until they're about 10 knots from the harbor and then we detonate the bombs we planted inside them beforehand. The biggest problem is their aircraft. We will have to preemptively take care of those first. Which is where Louie comes in. Thanks to his study of Aeronautics Engineering, he can sabotage the planes causing them to crash 5 minutes after launching. Jackson and Laura will be coming with me in order to lead the frontal assault. Hugh and Fiona will infiltrate the Nazis' boats and place the bombs. Everyone else will be assisting in the assault. We can't let what happened to poor Lenny happen to anyone else."

Everyone took a moment of silence to lament the loss of Lenny, one of the previously last surviving Jews before 2 months ago when the Nazis caught him and publicly executed him as an example. The rebellion leader lifted his head up and ordered his troops to move out.

Everyone grabbed a myriad of different weapons which included a variety of rifles and machine guns that the group has been smuggling for the past 2 years now thanks to the help of the local mafia. Everyone geared up and went to their assignments.

Louie along with two other soldiers, one male and one female, went over to the Waterloo Crescendo Air Strip/hanger. Louie is a short, pale man who is more geared for technical work than actual military duty. The two soldiers put mufflers on their rifles and shot at the two Nazis guarding the door. A third one just happened to be walking by at the time and saw them die but he was shot down before he could call for backup. The soldiers dragged the dead soldiers out of sight and stole their clothes. Louie already came in an engineering outfit in order to blend in. They opened the door into the building containing several aircraft. For now, it was unoccupied, and Louie quickly got to work. It took two hours in order to sabotage all the planes but once that was said and done, they gave the all clear on their burner phone.

Simultaneously, Hugh and Fiona were in their Nazi military uniform onboard one of the many vessels. Hugh is a tall, toned black man with hazel eyes who walks with an air of authority around him while Fiona is a slightly shorter and slightly tanned white woman with blond hair and green eyes who serves as his second in command. Prior to joining the rebellion, Hugh and Fiona initially worked for the Nazi army fully buying their propaganda that they were constantly airing all the time. However, during their time served they witnessed unspeakable acts of atrocity against humanity that showcased how vile Hitler's ideology was. The first time was enough to make Hugh run out of the room and barf in the nearby toilet. Him and Fiona shared the same sentiments about the crimes against humanity the Nazis were committing which later blossomed into love. They have been engaged three months now and they plan to host their wedding after the mission if all goes according to plan. Thanks to their ranks in the army, Hugh himself being a general they were allowed to access any part of the ship that they so desired, without question. This made it easy to apply the C4 in all the ships in remote rooms nobody would ever think twice about. It took them about an hour to finish their "inspections", but upon completion he and Fiona saluted their fellow soldiers and walked away. Once they were out of sight and earshot, Hugh took out his burner phone and gave his "all clear".

The commander of the rebellion, Jason DiMartino hung up his phone and turns around to his troops.

"Men, for far too long those Nazi bastards have been committing mass genocide left and right ever since World War 2. It started with the Jews, but that wasn't enough for them. So they started targeting people of other faiths, ethnicities, and even sexual orientation. The only thing keeping them from exterminating us completely is the sheer lack of manpower on their side. Well, I say no more! Let's go kick some Nazi ass and revive the name of America!"

The army cheered and Jason led them towards the dock. They started out by throwing grenades in the battlefield creating a huge smokescreen. Gunfire could be heard everywhere as the shots coming from the smokescreen hit several Nazis knocking them down with blood leaking from their gunshot wounds. The Nazis start scrambling onto the docks and return fire. One rebellion soldier gets out a machine gun and starts making short work of several soldiers. Jason advances out of the smokescreen and fires at several Nazi soldiers. Plenty of their own men are being gunned down by the Nazis with several causalities on their side as well. Jason walks back into the smoke as odd green balls roll into the Nazi forces. The rebels put on their gas masks as the tear gas sprays from the balls. This makes it very tough for them to aim. The admiral in charge issues an air strike.

The planes leave the hangars and quickly go down to the docks but upon reaching them the engine blows out in every single one of them. The pilots eject themselves as the planes crash in the ocean narrowly missing the boats and one on the dock. The rebellion runs as the plane crash lands setting off a massive explosion. They quickly run into a nearby building behind some crates as the explosion completely decimates the dock blasting apart the windows of the warehouse setting off a chain reaction that detonated all the bombs on the ships at once destroying them. The cloud from the explosion could be seen in all of Waterloo Crescendo. No Nazis survived. Not every rebellion soldier made it to cover. Jason walks out of the warehouse surveying the blaze that was once the Waterloo docks. They won, but at what cost?

*<End of The Butterfly Effect>*

# The Superheroes

## Side Mission: The Frozen Prisoner

Inside an orbital base above Earth's atmosphere, the boss hangs up a transmission to Jeremiah and Hurricane. Once the transmission is over, he commands, "Computer. Recommend sector to capture Icy Pete."

On the screen above him in front of his desk, it begins speeding through sector numbers until it stops on Sector 22. Once the sector was selected, he dials them up. Their leader Colossal Boy (a young adult with messy black hair and yellow eyes), who was conveniently sitting in front of the monitor of his sector's computer, answers the transmission bringing their boss on the computer's screen.

"Hello. This is Colossal Boy, leader of Sector 22. How may I be of service?"

"I got a mission for Sector 22. Call the rest of your team right away before I give you the details."

"Roger." He salutes before slamming down a button sounding an alarm. A microphone rises out of the control panel in front of him. "Sector 22! Report to the conference room immediately! I repeat: 'report to the conference room immediately.'"

A redhead wielding a welding torch turns it off and lifts up the mask as a burly black dude (Han, muscle) runs past her. A chair slides out from deeper in the base and a young man with blond hair and glasses attempts to jump off it while moving (Dex, brains). However, he lands face-first on the floor knocking aside his rounded glasses. He picks them up, puts them back on, and stands up. He runs to the conference room. The redhead puts down the wielding torch and runs past her boombox to the conference room (Susan, negotiator). When she arrives, a big tall black woman says to her, "Glad you could make it Susan." (Bertha, stealth).

Colossal Boy double-checks to make sure his entire team has assembled, and once confirmed he says to the boss, "Everyone has arrived."

"Alright, let's begin. Your mission is to capture the notorious villain, Icy Pete." A picture of her in a purple parka with orange hair partially frozen and yellow eyes appears on screen. He continues, "and bring her to Superhero HQ 5, alive."

Colossal Boy interrupts him, "Hold up. You're sending us to capture one of the most dangerous supervillains on the planet and you want us to bring her in, alive? Couldn't we just kill her?"

Everyone looks at him in horror while understanding his sentiments. They turn back to the boss on screen.

"I understand your concern, but we have just learned it may not even be her fault. Here's the gist of it. We have recently learned that several of these artifacts (Golden orbs with smiling faces appearing on screen approaching Earth) that we are dubbing 'Evil Orbs' have landed on Earth and what's worse: a few of them have traveled back in time creating these seven villains. (Seven bios fill the screen with the likes of Icy Pete and John known for his pyrokinesis along with five others. Suddenly the screen switched to a wireframe model and a 3D rendering of an Evil Orb.) These Evil Orbs have the ability to enter a host body (The Orb model unleashes a red energy trail and hops into the wireframe model) and infect, or rather corrupt, them (the wireframe model turns completely red). Because of this, we must assume that anyone in possession of an Evil Orb has no free will of their own and cannot be held accountable for their actions. (The screen switches back to the boss.) That is what's going on."

"That sounds completely nuts," loudly states Bertha.

"I am not going to deny your statement on this regard, and I'll go so far as to agree with it. The fact of the matter is that this is happening, and we got to deal with a lot of variables. Any further questions?" the boss asks.

Colossal Boy asks, "The name 'Evil Orbs' seems to imply that there are 'Good Orbs'. If we just learned of these things, why are we calling them 'Evil Orbs' and not just 'Orbs'?"

The boss answers, "You are correct in assuming there is a Good Orb."

"Good Orb? Singular?" questions Colossal Boy.

"Yes, the good orb, as we are calling it just the 'Orb' has recently been found prior to our discovery of the Evil Orbs and has come into the possession of one 'Jeremiah Ellison' (A picture of him appears on screen), who is now the current leader of Sector 17."

"He's a kid? You put him in charge of a sector?" loudly voices Dex.

"I've already tested him and he has proven his capability in combat," says the boss on this manner.

As Dex vocalizes his concern on the age of Jeremiah, Colossal Boy stares at the picture, sweating a bit. He licks his lips hungrily before shaking it off.

"The matter of Jeremiah is irrelevant to the mission other than he's the best bet of destroying the Evil Orbs. Any further questions or concerns about this matter can be filed after the mission. Does everyone understand?" states the boss.

They reluctantly nod yes.

"Good. End transmission."

The boss hangs up. Colossal Boy slaps his cheeks, turns to face his teammates, and yells, "Sector 22, report to duty." They cheer in response. They load up on the airship and take off. Using the data sent to them, they have no problem tracing the whereabouts of Icy Pete. They arrive at the base of Icy Pete and land a fair distance away from the base. Upon landing, they launch some probes to scout out the base. The base itself was a cave with two male guards standing in front of it. Inside the cave was a few tables, crystals of ice, a tv, and a wall of ice in front of one of the doors.

Colossal Boy begins, "Here is the plan. Dex will disable the security system in order to maximize stealth. Once disabled, Bertha will infiltrate the base, and procure us disguises. Once we successfully infiltrate the hideout, Han will break the ice and create a distraction while I move in and capture Icy Pete." He looks at Han and says to him specifically, "And Han, don't fall for her charm. Remember, duty before gals."

"I know," replies Han dejected.

"Lastly, we'll need to escape with the prisoner in tow. This is where Susan comes into play. Since most of the guards appear to be male, Susan will go in and charm them to let us through without a single question. If successful, we'll return to the ship and take off. Does everyone understand the plan?"

"Sir, yes, sir."

"Alright, then everyone move out!"

Everyone got into position. Dex found the circuit breakers and cut the power. Han and Colossal Boy grab the guards in front and knock them out. Bertha runs in there. She quickly jumps up and clings to the ceiling, crawling across it like a spiderwoman. Colossal Boy puts on his disguise. Han tries putting his on, but it rips thanks to his physique. Bertha continues crawling across the ceiling until she spots two XL guards having a conversation. She shoots webbing and tows one of the XL guards up and knocks him out by drugging him with some tablet. The other one says, "Huh?" before webbing grabs him too and he is drugged unconscious. She webs them up good and proceeds into an unoccupied room. The door closes and she jumps down with a thud. She quickly puts on one of the uniforms as some guards outside were talking.

"Did you hear that?"

"Yeah, but it was probably nothing."

"It sounded like something crashed."

"Probably a baby-sized earthquake?"

"A baby-sized earthquake localized entirely in the confines of one room?"

"Yes."

The guard looks at the other one in disbelief behind his mask.

"I'm checking it out."

"You do that."

One of the guards walks off as a third guard chimes in, "I see why you dropped out of school."

"Oh come on! Nothing was happening there."

The other guard opens the door and sees the disguised Bertha next to a bunch of knocked down furniture.

"What happened here?"

Bertha replies, "I tripped and accidently knocked over this furniture. It was not a pretty sight."

"Well clean it up. You know how Pete is when she's disturbed."

As he walks out, he mumbles to himself, "I swear why did I ever join this place?"

He closes the door behind him. Bertha breathes a sigh of relief. She picks up the furniture she purposely knocked down as a ruse to avoid suspicion and once it was picked up, she left the room. Colossal Boy is outside, in his disguise impatiently tapping his foot. Bertha walks out of the cave, takes off her helmet to let them know it's her, and gives Han his disguise. He puts it on, and they walk in.

Colossal Boy quietly asks Bertha, "Have you found anything yet?"

"Only that Pete hates being disturbed," whispers Bertha.

"I see. Well, keep an eye and ear out."

She nods before walking off. They walk over to the wall of ice. Standing in front of it Colossal Boy says, "Well Han once we break this thing, every guard in here will be on our tail. You ready?"

He nods. Colossal Boy makes a spiral of flames all around him condensing into a fireball. Han punches the ice at the exact moment the fireball is launched at it shattering the ice, the sound echoing across the entire cave. All the guards stand up and run straight at them, except the dropout. He fell asleep. Too much booze. Han turns around and charges at them punching the first one in range as Bertha shoots a web and flings a guard into the wall behind her. Colossal Boy rushes in the room and slams the door behind him. A sudden blizzard blows inside the room in a spiral as spikes of ice surround him with the sound of rapidly freezing water vapor present during the act.

"Who are you? Identify yourself!" demands Icy Pete the blizzard intensifying.

Colossal Boy spins around flames igniting all around him breaking the ice creating shattering sounds all around him. He flies up in the air and declares, "The name is Colossal Boy. Don't you dare forget it!" Fire appears in his hands and he firmly grasps it in one palm before opening it and firing a huge blast towards Icy Pete. The blizzard intensifies further as the sound of water vapor freezing rapidly echoes throughout the room as the fire comes in contact with a wall of ice. Icicle spears rush towards Colossal Boy from the side at breakneck speed. He quickly axe kicks in mid-air with fire trailing his motion shattering the ice. He shoots a current of electricity where the spikes came from and shocks Pete. Pete falls on her knees as the blizzard subsides clutching her heart. Colossal Boy lands as Pete outstretches her other hand and a flurry of snow shoots out of it towards Colossal Boy. He makes his own wall of ice to block it, but it instantly cracks. He starts running close to the speed of sound around the ice circling the room. He slams into Icy Pete causing her to bounce across the floor. Colossal Boy runs his finger across his face and feels a wrinkle that wasn't there before. He looks rather annoyed and angry. Ice forms a barrier around Icy Pete filling the room with more sound similar to glass shattering. He runs, albeit a bit slower this time, and punches a hole through the ice. A spike stabs him in the chest. The spike breaks as he staggers backwards. Colossal Boy removes the ice spike from his chest looking at it worryingly before it starts healing breathing a sigh of relief. He hears rambling, "I hate the cold. Why does it always have to be so cold?"

This naturally confuses him. The blizzard reignites all around him obscuring his vision. More ice spikes start heading his way and he jumps backwards flying upwards to avoid them. The blizzard gets thicker. "So cold. Too cold. Just warm me up, please!" Icy Pete's eyes start glowing glacial blue and the blizzard kicks into a frenzy. Colossal Boy feels himself freezing alive as the blizzard reaches a fever pitch. Ice forming along all the walls. There were several new wrinkles on his skin as it slowly lost its luster. His hand ignites in a giant flame and he flies head first directly towards the barrier at inhuman speed and shatters it. He clasps his hand together, puts them over his head, and hits her with them causing her vision to fade as she loses consciousness.

Susan already negotiated with the guards as Colossal Boy kicks open the door. "We need to get out of here now!" They start running but before Susan leaves one of the guards asks her, "Are we still on for Bridge at Tuesday?" She answers, "You know it," while running away. They load up onto their airship and set a course for Superhero HQ 5.

. . .

Sector 22 are in their ship's prison block asking Icy Pete questions.

Susan asks, "Question 1: why is your name Icy Pete?"

"Icy represents my ice powers. Pete is the name my parents gave me. They wanted a son, but instead ended up with a daughter. They took out their frustration by naming me Pete," answers Pete.

"Why?" asks Susan.

"Because parental torture is temporary, a name is forever," answers Pete.

Everyone grimaces before Susan says, "That is sad."

"I'm not sure what to say about how screwed up that is. So let's move on to the next question," states Colossal Boy.

Han blurts out, "Do you have a boyfriend?"

"Han!" exclaims the rest of Sector 22 simultaneously.

"What?" asks Han confused.

Pete giggles and says, "Well, aren't you sweet?"

Colossal Boy walks Han over to the side and says to him, "Han, what did I say before?"

"Duty before gals," answers Han with the disappointment audible in his voice.

"Good."

He walks back up to the crowd and says, "Any further questions?"

Susan turns back to Pete on the other side of the red laser bars. "Do you have any undergoing plans we should be aware of?"

She shakes her head. She says lowering it with a look of despair visible on her face, "No. I just want to stay warm." The floor freezes around her.

Colossal Boy blurts out, "You got ice powers? Why do you need to stay warm?"

She gets up suddenly. A blizzard forms in the cell as she yells, "These powers are the reason I need to stay warm." Her entire cell freezes over. She curls up into a ball and stammers, "Nobody understands me. Nobody ever understands me." The blizzard continues as the cell continues to ice over with the ice gradually getting thicker. "If I can never be warm, I'll make it the same for everyone else." Even more layers of ice form on the cell wall. "I'll freeze the entire world if I have to." She looks at them and her eyes were glowing glacial blue. The ice starts creeping out of the cell. Dex slams against a button and the cell fills with green knockout gas. Pete falls unconscious.

"Well, that's all the questioning we can do at the moment. Everyone is dismissed." Everyone gets up and leaves, all but Colossal Boy, his eyes hidden in the shadow of his hair. His yellow eyes train themselves on Icy Pete.

The door opens again, and Susan asks, "Are you coming?"

"Yeah, I'll be right there," answers Colossal Boy.

Susan walks away and Colossal Boy looks at Pete and says, "I'll have to drain you a little bit later." He scoffs as his stomach growls. He looks at his hands more wrinkled than ever. Colossal Boy walks out with one last look at the prisoner before leaving.

Colossal Boy walks up to the bridge. He hears while seeing Susan turn bright red, "I do not!"

Bertha says to her, "Come on girl, just admit it!"

"There is nothing to admit," says Susan crossing her arms.

"Did I miss something?" asks Colossal Boy.

"Ah, Colossal Boy. Perfect timing. We need to settle a bet. Would you date Susan?" asks Dex.

Colossal Boy turns beet red but quickly composes himself, "Who wouldn't want to date her? I mean, she's got a nice-"

The alarms suddenly go off before he can finish that sentence. Dex runs off to the control panel and checks the source of the alarm, to which a fuel gauge appears on screen. "It appears we're out of fuel."

"Oh great," says Colossal Boy before the ship starts falling.

Colossal Boy runs to the side and opens the door before jumping out of the ship. He flies in front of it and tries to stop it in mid-air. It crashes into him and pushes him down. Using his flight combined with super strength he exerts force in order to stop its descent. It weighs heavily on him in every sense of the world as his muscles tighten and contract in order to fulfill this impossible task being enhanced by an unknown energy deep within his stomach. It slows down and eventually stops in mid-air. He lands in a heavily forested area and places the ship down. He drops to his knees gasping for air. His entire body looking even more ragged. His hand shakes as he gazes at the new wrinkles on it.

His team run out of the ship. Colossal Boy asks, "Is everyone…alright?"

They all look at each other talking amongst themselves with a ton of nodding before they look at Colossal Boy and nod their head.

"Good. Dex, do we have any spare fuel?"

"Yeah, it's in the back. I can have this ship back in the air in 20 minutes."

"Good. I'm going to check on the prisoner. I'll be right back."

Colossal Boy hurriedly walks into the ship and over to the prison block. The door opens and he peers into the cell to see Icy Pete still breathing. He says, "Good. This is a golden opportunity. For shame, you have to die but your powers will not go to waste."

His stomach growls and he places his palm on it before stretching it towards Icy Pete. He shoots a golden beam from his hand and it envelops Susan. His body starts reverting to its former splendor as he breathes a sigh of ecstasy. Pete has no clue what's going on since she's still unconscious. All of a sudden, the beam turns red catching Colossal Boy off guard. He suddenly experiences pain in his chest. He starts screaming and yelling, "What is this energy? It's so massive and unstable." He screams again. Susan hears him along with Dex and they run to the prison block. The connection breaks and Colossal Boy drops to his knees as the red energy forms a red energy dragon and roars at him. Susan and Dex arrive at the scene to witness the red energy dragon. It rushes out of the room phasing through the wall roaring even louder. The energy leaves Pete. Her body goes limp. The dragon escapes. Once outside, the dragon gains mass and density as it turns snow white becoming solid looking very much like a Chinese dragon. It roars once again. Snow starts falling over the forest. Han looks up and sees the giant dragon in the air. It unleashes a breath of ice upon the ship and freezes it solid before flying away. Han runs to the ship's door now barricaded by ice. He punches the ice making a dent in it. In the prison block, Susan asks, "What happened?"

"I don't know. I went to check on Pete and next thing I know, some weird dragon comes out of her," answers Colossal Boy a little confused himself.

Dex chimes in, "Everyone, you might want to take a look."

They look at Pete's lifeless body and come to the realization that she's dead. And to think Colossal Boy didn't get to drain all of her energy. Ok, now I feel a bit weird. They help Colossal Boy up and head out of the prison block. They see the ice on the window.

"Oh crap," says Colossal Boy.

He runs to the door and sees the frozen exit. He orders, "Dex, get this ship fueled ASAP. We need to get airborne as soon as possible!"

Dex salutes and runs into the hallway.

"Susan, we need to get this ice melted. There should be a flamethrower in the back. Grab it so we can use it."

She salutes and runs into the hall. Bertha lands behind Colossal Boy with a big thud.

"I honestly thought you were out there with Han."

"So did he," replies Bertha.

"Right, help me break this ice."

Bertha charges at it and punches it. Colossal Boy's tries to ignite his hand, but it's only sparks compared to the other times today and he can't keep it alight. He punches the ice. Susan makes it to the back and sees the flamethrower on the side of a crate. She grabs it and runs out of there. Colossal Boy punches the ice but his flames die out. He looks at his hand irritatingly. He decides to do it the old-fashioned way. Susan is running across the hall with the flamethrower and some picks and hammers on a belt around her. She makes it and sees Colossal Boy and Bertha. She clears her throat and they step aside. Han sees the flamethrower and steps back. She lights it up and it fires full blast towards the ice melting it slowly. It breaks through and Han rushes back on to the ship. They all look at each other and nod before rushing back to the bridge.

Colossal Boy activates his Emergency Watch in order to contact Dex. "Is the ship ready to launch?"

"Just about. It'll take a couple of more minutes."

Colossal Boy sighs putting his hands to his temple as he sits down and says, "Alright. Let me know when it's done."

He hangs up and the watch closes. In a couple of minutes, Dex finishes fueling up the ship and it lifts off after the dragon. Sector 22 takes the time to discuss a plan against the dragon. They catch up to the dragon in no time. The sides of the ship open up, breaking off some of the ice, revealing missiles. They fire and hit the dragon now screaming in pain. Colossal Boy in a jetpack opens the side door and says, "I should have a few minutes of flight before it fizzles out. I'm going to attract that dragon's attention while Bertha goes on its back and delivers the payload. Understood?"

"Understood," says Han and Bertha simultaneously.

Colossal Boy puts on some goggles and jumps out of the ship backwards and flies up to the dragon. It shot its ice breath at the missile launcher freezing the missiles. Alarms are going off in the ship's bridge. Dex exclaims, "We can't fire any more missiles."

Colossal Boy heard that from his watch's speaker. He yells, "Hey dragon!" The dragon looks at him. "You're the ugliest creature I've ever seen!" The dragon lunges at him. Colossal Boy flies upward to avoid its attack. A blizzard emanates from its body reducing Colossal Boy's visibility. An ice ball suddenly hits him sending him flying in the air. He headbutts the ice ball breaking it in half. Bertha and Han are on the roof of the airship.

"You ready?" asks Han.

"I was born ready," smugly replies Bertha.

Han picks her up and tosses her at the dragon. She grabs on to its tail and it roars. It squirms and shakes in all directions even flying in a perfect circle in an attempt to shake her off. Bertha climbs up the dragon as Colossal Boy shoots out of the blizzard and punches the dragon in the chin. This angers the dragon and it attempts to freeze Colossal Boy who makes his own ice sphere to shield himself. Susan is inside the ship working on breaking the ice on the missiles enough to fire them. She finished one and says into her watch, "Missile 1 ready to fire."

Bertha says into her watch, "This is Bertha. Hold your fire. I'm on the dragon."

Dex reports, "Roger that. I will hold off all remaining fire."

Colossal Boy melts his ice sphere and makes icicles out of thin air. He launches them at the dragon hitting its eyes, below its neck, and on its waist. The dragon roars in pain. It aims its attention at Colossal Boy and shoots a blizzard straight from its mouth at him. He braces for impact. Bertha jumps on the icicles, vaulting off the second one, climbing off the third one before landing on top of the dragon's head. She lights a stick of dynamite and tosses it into the dragon's mouth. It explodes. Bertha starts falling and Colossal Boy swoops in and catches her. However, his flight starts failing. Bertha turns on the jetpack and they fly back into the ship. The dragon's remains vanish into red energy as they close in on Superhero HQ 5 spying a crude-looking rocket flying past them.

They dock in the hangar and exit the ship, turning around to examine the damage. Hurricane walks up to them. "Glad to see you could make it. Unfortunately, you just missed Jeremiah." He looks at the ship. "Icy Pete must have given you a lot of trouble. It's going to be an interesting report to read."

Colossal Boy smiles and says, "Yeah, I suppose it will be."

# Side Mission: The Wrath of Whirlwind

"Computer. Recommend sector for the apprehension of Whirlwind!" dictates the boss.

The computer rapidly scrolls through the many different entries on its screen until it lands on Sector 38. The boss sits on his chair and dials them up. On the other side of the line, Force, leader of Sector 38, answers.

"Yell-o. This is Sector 38. Force speaking."

The boss now on screen replies, "This is your boss speaking. I got a mission for you."

Force jumps enthusiastically, "Sweet. Are you finally sending us on a search for the Amazon Crystal?"

The boss answers awkwardly, "Umm…no. Why do I have to keep telling you that it disappeared along with Sector 41?"

"Until we believe you," answers Force smugly.

The boss is so done with this so he just says, "Just get Brain and Brawn over here so we can get started."

"Roger," says Force.

He gets up scooting the chair and leaves the room for a brief moment. Upon his return, he comes with a young woman the same age as him named Brain and a slightly taller muscular man named Brawn.

Upon entering the room, Brain instantly asks the boss, "Are you finally going to send us to search for the Amazon Crystal?"

"Yeah, are you?" echoes Brawn enthusiastically.

The boss smacks himself in the forehead and sighs softly. Afterwards, he replies taking a deep breath first, "Like I told Force, no. Seriously, what's with your obsession over the Amazon Crystal?"

Force answers, "It's a very powerful artifact that must be kept out of the wrong hands at all costs." Then he switches to a softer tone of voice for the rest of his statement, "Plus, we can't return home without it."

"Which was why we insisted that you give us the crystal, but noooo! You had to give it to Sector 41 instead," complains Brain.

The boss says softly, "I had no idea. We can't change the past (not yet at least), but we can change the future." He changes back to his regular tone of voice, "Now I got a mission for the three of you."

Brawn pumps himself up and says, "Let's do this!"

"Your mission to go capture the notorious villain Whirlwind. According to our intelligence and satellite tracking, he is currently operating in Tokyo, Japan. More specific coordinates will be sent to you…now."

Force's Emergency Watch blares and he presses the button opening it up revealing a blinking red spot somewhere on the streets of Tokyo.

"However, we are receiving some kind of technical interference inside the general area, so once you're there. You're on your own. Once captured, you are to bring him to Superhero HQ 5, alive. Understood?"

Force salutes, "Yes, sir. Understood."

"Good. Now be on your way."

The boss hangs up and the team turn around and rush to their small one-man airships, hopping into the cockpit of each one setting a course for Tokyo. In the span of several minutes, they reach their destination: Tokyo, Japan. As they land on the street, a powerful gust of wind blows in between the building blowing their airships into the nearest building. They slam a button on their dashboards quickly opening up their cockpits and ejecting them right before their ships explode. The skyscraper starts falling down onto the street. Force gets up and hops out of his chair. Brain assists him by controlling the speed of his descent via telekinesis. He turns a knob that acts as the outer edge of his belt's center piece before pressing smack dab in the center of it generating a big force field that engulfs him and the civilians in it. The skyscraper crashes down but the field remains intact, albeit buried under rubble. Brawn's chair finally lands, and he rushes over to the scene and tosses the debris aside, working on getting Force out of there. Brain lands and gets up. Her eyes start glowing blue and more rubble floats off of them and is tossed to the side. Force, now uncovered, deactivates the force field. The citizens crowd around them thanking them for saving their lives. Force makes it sound like it's no big deal while the other two kind of laugh at how he's handling it. It takes a few minutes, but the civilians finally leave. Force turns to the other two and asks, "So any idea what happened?"

Brain analyzes, "As we were getting ready to land, the wind got a lot stronger all of a sudden pushing our ships into the building forcing us to eject since our fuel tanks were ruptured."

Brawn asks the important question, "But why?"

Brain shakes her head holding her hands up high, "I don't know."

Force activates his Emergency Watch and pulls the profile on Whirlwind.

"Crazy thought, but it may have been Whirlwind. According to this, he has the ability of wind manipulation. Considering our crash has everything to do with the wind, it is highly likely he knows we're here."

The whole explanation confused Brawn as he is clutching his head trying to process everything. Brain translates, "In other words, be weary of the wind. It may be him." After that explanation, he finally gets it and simply says, "Oh."

Force says, "While we're here. I noticed that everyone was primarily speaking Japanese and I really had no clue what they were saying earlier."

Brain snarks, "Then why did you look so embarrassed?"

Brawn chuckles.

Force answers, "I assumed based on context clues. Anyway, we should get out the Universal Translators before we leave."

Brain gets a remote out of her pocket saying, "On it" and presses a button on it. Behind them, a sort of rectangular pipe emerges from the ground and it constructs itself on a hinge at the halfway point titling the rest of it at a 45° angle. It turns on its hinge and launches red discs in all four directions that land at different ends of Tokyo where bolts to attach them come out of the four corners of the disc and stick themselves into the ground before activating creating a field that auto-translates any language into the native language of the listener that spreads over a 10-mile radius.

Brawn questions, "Why do we need such big discs for the translators anyway? Wouldn't it be easier to just put it in our watches?"

Force answers, "An excellent question, and I'd like to agree with you on that. But when I went to ask about it, they said something about the circuitry being too complex at this time to effectively integrate it into the Emergency Watch. Which I question, but we can't do anything about that."

Brawn scratches his head and Brain chimes in, "Come on, let's go. We got a lot of work ahead of us."

Force nods and they start walking through the city. The city is bustling with activity with people walking as far as the eye can see. It doesn't take long for them to reach Shibuya. However, the wind suddenly shifts into a frenzy spiraling around them. The wind blows so strongly that it becomes visible forming a tornado in the middle of Shibuya directly in front of them. They stare at the tornado awe struck.

"How the heck do we defeat a tornado?" shouts Force in disbelief.

"You got me," responds Brain.

"But you're the brains of the operation," loudly snaps back Force.

Brawn pleas, "Come on you two. Stop arguing."

They both snap looking at Brawn, "Stay out of this Brawn!"

The tornado shifts towards them, the fierce winds pulling them. They stand their ground as long as they could with every fiber of their being, but the wind is too strong, and they are sucked into the tornado. They are at least 15 ft apart from each other. "Brain!"

"On it!" Her eyes start glowing and blue outlines appear around Force and Brawn as they yanked towards her. Quickly closing the distance, they are now gathered together in a group. The G-Force of the wind pressure starts crushing them. Force presses the button on his belt and a big spherical force field generates around them alleviating some of the pressure. He turns the outer edge of his belt shrinking the field down so there's just enough room for the three of them. They swirl around in the tornado until an unusual wind launches them out of it straight through a side. They bounce from building to building like a pinball machine until they eventually bounce down to the ground where Force deactivates the force field and they land on their faces.

Brain thanks, "Thanks Force. That gives me an idea. Maybe I can use my telekinesis to make a counter-tornado to cancel out the first tornado." The tornado starts moving further into the city homing in on them.

"We better make it fast, that tornado is heading right towards us," states Brain.

"How fast can you make it?" asks Force quickly.

"A couple of minutes," answers Brain.

"Got it. In that case I got an idea. Brawn, I need you to throw us at the tornado. Can you do that?"

Brawn flexes his muscles and brags, "No problem. You two are a breeze to lift."

Brain hops on Force's back holding on to him for dear life, her hands over his chest. Brawn picks them with both hands and gets ready to toss them. He yells, "Hold on tight!" In a quick motion of his arms, he tosses them towards the tornado at an angle that will insure they can come in contact with a building. All according to Force's plan. He presses the button on his belt and they bounce from building to building in zig-zags. They bounce straight into the tornado where the spiraling winds cause them to fly in the same direction of the tornado's rotation. Brain's eyes glow as she manipulates the air around her to make it swirl in the opposite direction creating a second tornado within the first one. The two tornadoes collide as the opposing forces slow them both down to a crawl until they dissipate into harmless air. With nothing holding them in the air anymore they start falling. Brain stops them right before they hit the ground. She puts them safely down, and Force deactivates the force field. Everyone nearby comes out of hiding and starts cheering for them.

Meanwhile in an undisclosed location,

"So, these people stopped my tornado, huh? Well, these fools have invoked my wrath. The wind will keep an eye on them," says ??? in Japanese. Good thing there were subtitles.

"Get out of here," shoos away ??? in Japanese.

Alright, I'm going. Geez.

***

Force, Brawn, and Brain are standing in the middle of a dark alley out of breath from running so much.

Force says in a huff, "*pant* *pant* We finally managed to escape the…crowd."

"Yeah. Let's *pant* *pant* catch our breath," agrees Brain.

"I'm with you there," echoes Brawn.

83

They plop down on the alley pooped from stopping a giant tornado and outrunning a crowd of grateful people. Force activates his Emergency Watch and tries to track Whirlwind using his energy signature, but to no avail. It only shows his general location and any attempts to zoom in are met with static.

"Stupid electrical interference," mumbles Force under his breath.

"How are we *pant* going to track Whirlwind anyway?" asks Brain.

"Don't know. I'm open to ideas," says Force.

Brawn suggests, "What if we make a giant sail and take that to his lair?"

Force shoots down crossing his arms, "No. He controls the wind, so for all we know he could send us all the way into a zoo and toss us into an alligator pit."

They go back to pondering this issue when it suddenly hits Brain. "Wait, I think Brawn is on the right track. Not necessarily with the giant sail, but if we can track the wind, we may be able to find him."

"Again, he controls the wind. Can't he make it blow from any direction?"

Brains wiggles her finger and "Tsk, tsk. If he's controlling the wind, there must be an origin point. That means that no matter the direction the wind blows, it must lead back to him."

Force, as much as he wanted to argue the point with her, could **not** think of a rebuttal. So he sighs in defeat and comments, "Gives a whole new meaning to the phrase, 'Go where the wind blows.'"

They get up and walk back to the wreckage of their ships. Since their watches are ill-equipped to track the wind, they gather a bunch of spare parts from the remains of their ship and started putting them together. Mostly Brain as she was the one who passed the Super-heroes tech course with flying colors. Eventually, they make a shoddy looking tracker with pieces of metal from the ship's debris, a radar screen that was surprisingly intact, and a piece of a weathervane they found lying around sticking it on top. Suddenly, a huge gust of wind knocked them down to the ground. However, this caused the new wind radar to pick up on the wind indicated by a trail of dots.

"Well, Brain. Looks like your idea hit the jackpot. Let's head out," says Force.

They get up, turn around, and start walking in the direction the wind came from following the trail from the radar. In the unknown location the shadowy figure says, "Drat. They're on their way here. This will not do. I might be able to turn those clouds above them into monsters if I try hard enough."

Back at Sector 38's location, they stopped to wait for more wind to blow. However, the only wind that is blowing is the gentle breeze of a nice day. Sitting on a bench, Brain and Brawn are amusing themselves in a heated game of Tic-Tic-Toe. Brain cheers, "Tic-tac-toe. Three in a row!" "Argh!" screams Brawn in frustration. "Rematch," he declares. They start their 32$^{nd}$ round as Force looks up at the clouds. Suddenly, the wind blows ticking off the navigator as the clouds start making a strange formation. They start forming chubby humanoid bodies made out of the surrounding cumulus clouds swirling together. They open their puffy eye sockets. They fall down to Earth with a thud. He gets out a bola and starts twirling them before hurling them at one of the cloud monster's feet. Unfortunately, it went straight through it and hit the ground. Force remarks, "That's all I got. Hey, can you two help me out here?"

"Me and Brawn are a little busy at the moment. Can it wait?" complains Brain.

Force quickly speed walks there, takes the piece of paper from them, and tears it apart into confetti using his bare hands before letting go of it as the little shreds of paper fall. Normally, the wind would blow it away. Instead, the wind swirls and blows it all back together again.

"Oh, come on! Curse you Whirlwind!"

"Tic-Tac-Toe! Three in a row," declares Brain cheerily.

She looks around and notices they're now on the roof of a manga publishing company. Force noticing her confusion simply states, "I had to think fast, ok?"

Brain asks, "You do realize the monsters are made of clouds? So, we're probably in a lot more danger on a roof than on the ground."

The winds swirl once more as the clouds above them turn into cloud monsters. They land on the roof with their backs to the street.

"I wish that you didn't say anything," complains Force.

"It's not my fault that I'm so smart," sasses Brain crossing her arms in a huff.

Brawn comments, "Ah! You two are so cute when you're arguing like that."

Force orders, "Fight cloud monsters now, argue later!"

Force presses the button on his belt and a force field generates around him. Brain uses her telekinesis to go bowling using Force as her bowling ball as she propels him at the cloud monster's feet resulting in a strike. The cloud monsters fall down to the ground as Force starts bouncing around the buildings. Brain hops on Brawn's shoulders and he grabs hold of her and tosses her towards Force. Force deactivates his force field as Brain tosses a tracking device on him. Right before he hits a building he reactivates the force field but the sheer closeness of the time causes a split second between the activation and the bounce making it contort like a bubble about to burst causing it to change angles to a straighter shot that isn't losing altitude. Brawn jumps off the roof and proceeds to do a superhero landing on the ground creating a small crater on the impact sight. The two cloud monsters swirl together merging into one gigantic cloud monster. It goes in for a punch aimed at Brawn who simply turns sideways as it hits the road destroying it. One random citizen complains, "Why is it always a giant monster?" Good thing the translator is turned on. Brawn tears a nearby streetlamp out of the ground exposing the wires underneath as they snap apart. He succeeds in getting it out of the ground and holds it like a bat. Brawn swings at the cloud monster. Unfortunately, it goes clean through the giant cloud monster. It raises its foot and attempts to stomp on Brawn. Before it could accomplish its goal, it falls backwards squishing a few cars creating a new cloud monster-shaped hole in the street. Nobody was harmed during this fall except the monster.

Brawn looks ahead and sees Brain levitating overhead. He assumes that Brain hit it with a psychic blast. The cloud monster stands back up using its arms to pull itself back up. In frustration, it punches a building next to it knocking it over causing other buildings to fall like dominoes.

As the buildings' collapse shake the very earth, Brawn asks the important question, "How do we stop this thing?"

Brain answers as she gets out a teleport gun, "We don't. We teleport it to another location. Once it's out of Whirlwind's range, it should deform."

She checks the charges on the gun.

"We only have two charges left thanks to Force's quick thinking earlier. That means we only have one shot."

Brawn doesn't question how two charges equals one shot as Brain turns the knobs on the side entering the coordinates on it. The cloud monster goes in for another punch and Brain fires at it. It glows white and in a flash of light, it disappears. It reappears in a far-off open field on the other side of the world where it dissipates into ordinary clouds once more. Back at Tokyo, everyone was celebrating the monster's defeat. Brain uses her telekinesis to pick up Brawn and they levitate to a park to wait for the signal.

Meanwhile, Force is walking on a dark street as the wind blows gently. Looking at his radar, it points to the skyscraper in front of him. The source of the wind. He looks up but is unable to see the roof due to the thin layer of clouds above him. The wind is blowing up there, returning to its source. Force presses down on his tracking device changing its frequency.

Sitting down in the park, the frequency change registers in Brain's Emergency Watch as the blip on the radar turns from red to blue. They look at each other and nod. That was their que. Brain busts out the teleport gun with a twirl as Brawn grabs on to her. She aims it at them setting the coordinates with the knobs on the side and fires. They turn white and disappear. Their atoms rushing through an unseen path until reassembling in a flash of light at Force's location, right next to him.

Towering above them on the roof of the abandoned skyscraper sits a shadowy figure looking down at them through an old, worn out monitor in front of him. He curses, "Curses!" He slams his hand on his throne-like chair. "They have found me." He takes a deep breath as he puts his hand to his head shaking it in a nervous sweat. "I have to get rid of them! They're too efficient."

Wind starts swirling all around him at high speed, spreads out across the entirety of the tower, and accelerates down it. The radar picks up on it. "Whirlwind is attacking!" yells Force as the wind spiral touches ground right in front of them. They stare at the sudden spiral of wind before it spreads out violently knocking them over. They get up and Force yells, "Brain!" "On it!" Her eyes glow blue and a gate is opened in the wind stockpiling huge air pressure as its edge.

"Get in the building now!"

They run into the skyscraper. Whirlwind increases the force of the wind to incredibly dangerous levels putting pressure on Brain and increasing the air pressure stockpiling on the edge of the gate. Once inside she gets a sudden headache yelling in pain. Force runs up yelling, "Brain!" The air pressure is released and collides sending a massive burst of air all around breaking the windows and some of the wall. As the rubble and shattered glass hit the floor, the building starts shaking as the walls crack some more. A piece of the wall falls off as the wind rushes inside swirling around to make a mini tornado around them that crashes through the ceiling shattering it. The rubble begins to fall with a huge piece ready to crush them. Force activates his force field protecting them from the stone. The wind picks up threatening to blow them off the floor as more debris falls around them.

"Even if we stop the tornado, we'll be crushed by the building," observes Force.

Brain checks her Emergency Watch and says, "Even if this section of the building collapses, the upper structure should remain intact. However, that won't help us."

Another piece of debris hits them as the shaking gets worse.

"Brain, in case we don't make it out alive, there is something I want to tell you," says Force.

Brain asks with the utmost attention looking at Force, "What is it, Force?"

"I...I..."

There was a huge bang and the building's lower floors completely cave in. However, Force saw an opportunity with various pieces of rubble falling at different speeds. He says, "Hang on!" He runs and rolls the force field closer to the tornado's edge and purposely lets it pick them up. They swirl around the tornado and Force says, "I need a psychic blast at a 34° angle at the bottom of the force field in 3, 2, 1." Brain complies and they fly out of the tornado and bounce along the falling rubble to an upper floor. Or so they thought, but they crash through the window outside the skyscraper. The wind blows down at supersonic speed accelerating them at dangerous speeds towards the pavement. Brawn says, "Let me out. I have an idea." Force deactivates the force field. Brain tries to block the wind with her psychic abilities but she's having a really tough time with it as the air pressure builds in front of her. Brawn grabs Force and Brain and tosses them upwards towards the sky. The sudden shock caused Brain to lose concentration and the air pressure released hurtling Brawn down to the ground killing him. Brain yells,

"Brawn!' Force reactivates the force field and says, "Brain." Her eyes stained red with tears, she lets out a deafening scream and unleashes her most powerful psychic blast to date sending them up the skyscraper at ludicrous speeds where even the increased air resistance couldn't stop them. They shoot past the cloud cover and stop in midair just a little bit above the roof where they curve and fall down landing on it hitting it with such great force that they make a hole in it lodging themselves in it. Force deactivates the force field and Brain lifts them up to safety.

They see a monitor in front of them as a voice from behind it says, "So, you have finally found me." A figure stands up from behind it and walks out of the shadows revealing Whirlwind with dark eyes and white hair with a wind spiral pattern on his shirt.

"To think I almost had you. But no, you three, or I guess I should say you two, are the most persistent lot I've ever had the pleasure of dealing with."

"You killed Brawn!" yells Brain half sobbing.

"Did I? Who knows?" says the mysterious figure.

"Just to confirm, you are indeed Whirlwind, correct?" asks Force.

The mysterious figure laughs manically. "Yes, indeed I am." He starts walking towards them. "You two have been a thorn in my side all day and after you've come all this way just to see my face. Now that you have, I can't let you leave here alive!" He continues laughing manically.

They get into a fighting stance. Whirlwind stretches out his palm outward sending raging winds at them knocking them off balance and sending them off the edge of the building. Force activates his forcefield and Brain uses her telekinesis to make them circle around as a gust of wind blows past where they were heading down. They end up behind Whirlwind who goes to the edge of the building to make sure they're dead. Brain unleashes a psychic blast to launch themselves straight at Whirlwind. He hears them and looks behind him, but it's too little too late. They hit him off the building and he starts going into freefall. All of a sudden, the tornado from earlier, now full-sized, burst forth from the building destroying the wall causing the entire building to collapse. Force starts riding the tornado as Whirlwind controls the wind creating a smaller tornado to keep him still and afloat. The debris from the building is picked by the swirling wind and brought forth upward to them. Whirlwind blows a chunk of debris at them. Thinking fast, Force moves the field enough to launch themselves directly at it bouncing off it. He bounces off another one heading upward. Whirlwind makes air spears in the tornado and launches them at Force and Brain. Brain stops the spears and turns them around as they bounce off another piece of debris at an angle. She launches the spears at Whirlwind who dissipates them before they can make contact. However, that was a distraction. They hit Whirlwind head on knocking him out of the tornado.

Outside the tornado, they start falling. Whirlwind manipulates the wind in order to catch him as he stops in midair on top a wind cushion. Force and Brain land on the same cushion. Force deactivates the force field as Brain rushes at Whirlwind screaming in fury and agony. She starts jabbing at Whirlwind with a flurry of punches to which he blocks to the best of his abilities. She kicks him in the gonads causing him to wail in pain as he clutches his privates and falls to his knees. Unfortunately, this kick makes him lose concentration dissipating the wind cushion. They start falling once more. Force gets out a blaster and lines his shot. Originally, he aims at Whirlwind's head, but pauses for a brief moment. He adjusts his aim a bit lower and fires hitting Whirlwind in the chest. Force ends up next to Brain and activates his force field. They continue falling as Whirlwind is propelled upward.

Clutching his chest he yells, "You pretentious pricks! I will take great pride in watching you die."

They hit ground cracking most of the field but it held for a brief moment before shattering. Force is out of breath, his adrenaline not doing much to mask his exhaustion. Whirlwind gathers up air in the palm of his hand and uses it to form an air sword. Brain looks at

Brawn's lifeless body staining the street red. Next, Whirlwind prepares an air shield.

"Brain! Hit him now!"

No response.

"Brain?"

He looks and sees that Brain is out of the anger stage of grief and is now sobbing uncontrollably. Whirlwind uses the wind to lunge at them, specifically Brain. Force yells, "Brain!" as his legs run to intercept.

Brain looks up only to see Force sliced in the front as his force field could not activate in time. Once he falls, the field goes up supposedly trapping Whirlwind. However, he pushes the button on the belt and deactivates the field.

He says, "He's still alive. Barely, but he's still alive."

Whirlwind raises up his wind blade but Brain outstretches her palm and unleashes a psychic blast against him bouncing him across the road away from Force. Brain runs over to Force's body and removes the belt. She puts it on herself and gets into a fighting stance.

"You're the only one left girly. You think you're tough enough to fight me?"

She responds, "I know I'm tough enough to take you on."

The sword and shield dissipate and he sends a huge gust from above him straight at Brain who activates the force field shielding her but breaking the ground a bit. Her eyes glow blue a bit as she manipulates the wind. It circles around the spherical field right back at Whirlwind who waves his hands in front and spreads it thin. Brain uses a psychic blast and launches herself up at an arc attempting to crush Whirlwind under the field. Whirlwind blows the sphere away. Brain deactivates the field and quickly levitates at him going in for a punch. Whirlwind goes in for an air slice but Brain is on him too quickly and punches him in the face knocking out some of his teeth and causing him to spin and bounce off the ground. Panting with shorted breath, Whirlwind attempts to get up only to be pinned down by an unseen force. Brain levitating above him has her palm stretched forward straight at him, her eyes teeming with rage. Tears flow down her cheek as she considers the possibility of ending his life right then and there. However, she floats down and walks over to Whirlwind. She handcuffs him with special cuffs connected by a blue beam. Afterwards, she grabs a taser and knocks him out.

A while later, the Superheroes' prisoner transport ship arrives for Whirlwind. Its hatch opens and many heroes come out of the ship. They grab Whirlwind and load him up. Some heroes grab Force and take him inside to be treated. However, they confirm the worst about Brawn. Brain climbs aboard as they lift Brawn's remains into the ship. The hatch closes and the ship leaves for Superhero HQ 5.

Force begins to come to and Brain hugs him sobbing.

"I was…so…so worried."

"What about Brawn?"

"He's dead. No doubt about him…he's…dead."

Brain cries even harder. Force strokes her head hoping it will give her some relief.

# Mission 5: When Lightning Strikes

On a dark and stormy night at a power plant on the outskirts of New York City. Two workers are currently standing in front of a whirling, humming generator gauging and logging its electrical output as thunder roars from the outside.

"50 kilowatts yet again," says a male worker with straight black hair and glasses.

"As it should be. Quite frankly, you seem bored," comments the female worker with black hair tied in a bun.

"Aren't you? We do this day in and day out. And to what? Nothing ever changes," complains the man.

"Not on your shift," snarks the woman.

Lightning strikes the antenna from down below. Alarms sound throughout the entire plant as a yellow current of electricity travels quickly through the plant's wiring. The male worker checks the situation on his monitor and says, "There are abnormal power fluctuations happening throughout the entire plant."

"Shut the power down!" yells the female worker as the current enters the room and enters the generator. The electricity suddenly spikes as the generator whirls itself into overdrive sparking like a madman. The male worker is frantically typing at his keyboard, "I can't get this thing under control! What's going on here?"

The female worker on her own panel replies, "It looks like you got your wish."

The lights suddenly shut down and takes with it a section of New York City's power. All is silent in the plant except for the hum of the generator.

"I guess it's over."

Sparks fly from the generator as a screen above suddenly sparks to life adding a blue hue to the room. A yellow image with red eyes says on its speaker, "More. I, need, MORE!" More electricity flies out of the generator upon that declaration.

At Sector 17, Jeremiah and Tech Boy were having an argument about who's going to drive the Changing Rocket next mission.

"I built it! So I should get to drive it!" argues Jeremiah.

"And I'm telling you that I have more piloting experience so I should get to drive it!" logically argues Tech Boy.

Tech Girl sighs putting her palms to her head as she was looking at holographic projection of two clocks. One labeled "Earth" moving at a normal pace and one labeled "Gaxi" moving at a much slower pace. Taking her hand off her face, she turns around in her swivel chair and complains loudly, "Will you two stop arguing? I'm trying to do some work over here!"

Tech Boy comments, "Looks like you're just staring at clocks to me."

She slams her hands on the table getting up moving the chair behind her, the sounds of the wheels moving a bit across the floor. She turns around fuming with anger and stomps across the room in her big black boots over to Tech Boy. Once in front of him, she smacks him across the face turning his cheek red as his head moves at an angle due to the impact. Tech Boy, placing his hand across his reddened cheek sore from the blow, watches dumbfounded as Tech Girl marches off in a huff plopping down back on her chair. Jeremiah asks the very question on his mind after witnessing the scene, "Is that normal?" To which Tech Boy replies, "No."

The computer rings as a transmission comes in. Jeremiah rushes over taking a seat in his own swivel chair in front of the computer as Tech Boy and Tech Girl stand next to it, and he answers it. The boss shows up on screen and states,

"Sector 17. I have a new mission for you. Your mission is to go to a power plant at the outskirts of New York City and investigate the recent power outage. Due to a recent spacecraft crash, and multiple smaller outages in the area, we have reason to suspect possible villain activity on sight. I'm sending the coordinates now."

Their Emergency Watches sound off in alarm as their red light flashes from the button. They simultaneously press the button on their watches opening them up revealing the coordinates of the plant on the screen.

"We're on it!" states Jeremiah before ending the transmission.

Jeremiah presses a button on his Emergency Watch manifesting a green data sphere around him. His watch converts him into data turning him into a wireframe model as it downloads his civilian clothes. Once downloaded, it uploads his superhero uniform onto him manifesting on the 3D model. Once outfitted, the details of the model returns as he is materialized back into flesh and blood donning an oversized lab coat and boots as the data sphere recedes into his watch turning him into the inaccurately named Robot Boy. The three rush to the Changing Rocket and both Jeremiah and Tech Boy attempt to jump into the driver's seat. Instead, they end up pushing each other on the face. Neither budging on the issue, Tech Girl, already seated, had enough of this and pushes their faces aside.

"I don't have time to listen to your arguments, so just decide who's driving."

"As leader, I declare that I drive," decrees Robot Boy before hopping into the driver's seat.

Tech Boy groans and hops in himself before they take off.

In a matter of minutes, they arrive at New York where the day was overcast as they pass by the darkened buildings on the way to the power plant on the outskirts of the city. The rocket makes a low humming noise as it lands in front of the power plant. They all hop out of the rocket and walk to the door. Tech Boy tried opening the door but it was locked. He notices, "Strange. The security panel still has power to it." He ejects a wired circuit board out of his watch and connects it to the bottom of the panel. Afterwards, he runs a code cracking program in order to open the door. On the screen above the generator inside of the building, the yellow electrical mass on screen opens its eyes. The program cracks the first digit as Jeremiah watches enthusiastically.

He asks Tech Boy, "Hey could you possibly teach me how to do that?"

As the second digit was cracked, Tech Boy answers, "Yes. Actually, it's quite a simple process. First you-"

As he was talking, the security panel sparks a bit to no one's knowledge. The code cracker cracks the third digit as Jeremiah says, "Wow. But that seems kind of complicated."

"I can give you a more practical demonstration later."

"Yay!"

Tech Boy smiles at Jeremiah's enthusiasm as the code is cracked and the door unlocks. Jeremiah opens the creaking door revealing a dark hallway. Jeremiah looks at Tech Boy and Tech Girl as they activate their watch lights and walk into the plant. Jeremiah activates his and runs after them.

The lights of their watches casts a red hue across the dark hallway. Having caught up with Tech Boy and Tech Girl, Jeremiah walks overly cautiously behind them looking in every conceivable direction as they trudge across the dark, desolate, metallic hallway. Tech Boy notices this but continues walking deeming it as unimportant. A noise sounds further in the hallway like aluminum clanging against metal. Jeremiah unconsciously grabs the back of Tech Boy's lab coat. Tech Boy notices this and asks, "Are you scared?" Jeremiah nervously nods to which Tech Boy responds, "You have got to be kidding me. I'd thought you'd be a little more mature by human standards."

"Tech Boy!" snaps Tech Girl.

"What?" responds Tech Boy as yellow light fills the room mixing with the red hue from their watches. They look up and see electricity crackling from a wire overhead. A bolt of electricity strikes in front of them. "A warning shot," observes Tech Boy as he and his sister arm their blasters. They aim at the crackling electricity as a garbled voice warns through the speakers, "Leave, now!"

"State your business here!" declares Tech Boy.

"Food. Nothing more, nothing less."

Jeremiah lets go of Tech Boy's lab coat and stammers, "In the n-name of the S-Superheroes, we must ask you to v-v-vacate the p-p-premises."

Tech Boy states coldly, "Never show the enemy that you're scared!"

Tech Girl wants to snap at her brother for his statement, but couldn't muster up the resolve to contradict her own beliefs. The voice states, "Go away!" and fires off another warning shot before leaving.

The hall returns to a red hue lit up only by their Emergency Watches. Tech Boy goes deep in thought putting his head on his chin.

"I don't remember any alien species capable of controlling electricity. Jeremiah, is there any earth species that can control electricity?" asks Tech Boy analytical.

Jeremiah shakes his head. Tech Boy groans. "Well then, I don't know."

Tech Girl interjects, "Let's just go." She walks ahead and the others follow. Their footsteps echo across the hallway as they walk down it. Tech Boy speeds up his pace. When he was next to Tech Girl, she whispers, "What is your problem today?"

He whispers, "I don't know what you're talking about."

"Don't play dumb with me. You've been egging on Jeremiah all day. If you're not careful, they might send us back to our mother."

"Oh puh-lease. Even if I do that, I don't think we have anything to worry about. Besides, name one thing he's done worthy of being a leader."

Tech Girl was about to say something when their conversation was interrupted by the sound of a door opening.

Inside the room was a control panel in front of a windowed pane. Electricity crackles as the screen glows to life adding a blue hue to the room. In a far-off corner a red light powers on. Mechanical footsteps could be heard as a shambling heap of metal approaches them. Tech Boy and Tech Girl ready their blasters getting into a fighting stance. Jeremiah, scared out of his wit, leaps at it and strikes it with a whip of fire (Power: Fire Strike) scattering its pieces across the floor with several clangs. The panel starts playing audio.

"I can't get this thing under control! What's going on here?"

"It looks like you got your wish."

*Static*

"I guess it's over."

"More. I, need, MORE!"

Electricity suddenly fills the walls of the room filling it with a yellow hue as it pieces together the broken automaton. More shamble in behind Tech Boy and Tech Girl forcing them further into the room. They shoot them scattering parts across the floor, their impacts echoing across the whole room. They were being reconstructed as quickly as they were being destroyed with several more automatons, if you could call them that, being constructed all around them. Jeremiah looks at the robot zombies with a look of fear so terrifying that his eyes looked like they were going to pop out of his sockets. He starts breathing heavily dropping to his knees with his hands over his ears as his teammates continue shooting the mechanical abominations. However, no matter how many of them they tore to pieces, they just reassemble and continue onwards. Tech Boy looks in Jeremiah's direction as tears flows from Jeremiah's eyes before they start glowing blue. The place starts shaking as if a sudden earthquake hit the plant as air rushes towards Jeremiah, his whole body glowing blue. Thinking quickly, Tech Boy shoots the glass, grabs his sister, and runs, jumping out the shattered window. Jeremiah screams, "NOOOOOOOO!!!" as blue energy burst forth from his body decimating everything in its path like an explosion. What little glass was left of that window rushes outward with a boom. Tech Boy waits a couple of seconds as the room goes dark again.

He gets out a grappling hook, and latches onto the hole that was once a window. Tech Girl pulls out hers and does the same thing. They reel up their grappling hooks and see the total devastation of the room. The floor was barely there. The panel a heap of wires. All other sources of light were gone except the light from the trio's watches, and sitting there in a red glow was Jeremiah crying, on his knees, in the center of the room. Tech Boy looks at the state of the room, then at Jeremiah, and finally lands on his sister as he asks, "What is he? A living bomb?"

"Well…" responds Tech Girl before being interrupted by Jeremiah's watch alarm. He stands up, struggles to take a deep breath, and wipes away the tears before pressing the button. The operator's voice sounds, "Robot Boy, your power level suddenly spiked. What happened?"

Robot Boy looks around at the carnage caused by his outburst and responds, "I…don't know. The last couple of minutes…are a blur."

Tech Boy and Tech Girl walk behind Jeremiah into the operator's view, sort of, and Tech Boy states, "I'll tell you what happened. He suddenly exploded and destroyed the entire room he's in."

The operator replies with the screen of Jeremiah's power level appearing on his watch, "According to our data, he should not have reached critical mass yet.

"Critical mass? What are you talking about?"

"If Jeremiah's power level goes critical, he will explode and kill everything within a 5mi$^2$ radius."

Tech Boy steps back and yells, "So you're telling me that Jeremiah is A LIVING BOMB!?"

Then the realization dawns on him and he looks at his sister, "And you knew." He stomps towards her, grabs her shoulders, and shakes her violently, "Why didn't you tell me this sooner!?"

Tech Girl attempts to answer, "Well, I…umm." Tech Boy takes a deep breath, lets go of her, and angrily states, "You know what? It doesn't matter. I'm doing this mission solo." And he storms out of the room.

"I just…never had the chance to tell him," mumbles Tech Girl.

Tech Boy walks down the dark hallway, the only source of light: his watch. He thinks aloud, "I should have gone the other way. The generator was <u>literally</u> in the next room." Static crackles behind him and follows him. He hears it, draws his blaster, and fires at the source of the crackling, cutting a cable on the wall causing it to swing in front of him with exposed wires sparking. The sparks suddenly intensify and the electricity exits the wires and takes a somewhat humanoid form composed entirely out of electricity with red eyes.

"So, you're not just relegated to electrical appliances," states Tech Boy.

A much deeper and less distorted voice than earlier relies, "Didn't I tell you to leave earlier?"

Tech Boy aims his blaster straight at him. "Not until I run you out of this building."

"Pity. I have no quarrel against you. Turn back now and your life will be spared."

"That reminds me. Those two people in the video. What happened to them?"

"Gone. I gave them the same choice and they left."

"So, you didn't kill them?"

"No."

Footsteps could be heard from behind Tech Boy. In the distance a voice was calling, "…Tech Boy."

The electrical being's arm suddenly extends shocking Tech Boy. Tech Boy drops to his knees before hitting the floor. As his sight goes blurry, the electrical villain reenters the wires and rushes past Tech Boy right before he blacks out.

"Tech Boy, Tech Boy…"

Tech Boy begins to come to, but his sight is blurring. His ears are ringing. He can't make anything out.

"Tech Boy!"

Scratch that, now he can understand the voices. His vision slowly comes back as the blurry image takes on definitive shapes.

"Tech Boy, are you alright?" asks a feminine voice.

He recognizes the voice. His vision clears and he sees Robot Boy and Tech Girl, wracked with worry. Tech Boy gets up with a groan, his head still groggy from the attack.

"What happened?" asks Tech Boy, his hat fried from the attack.

"We were running after you and saw a huge flash of electricity," answers Tech Girl.

"Afterwards, you fell on the floor. Like…" Jeremiah makes a falling down motion with his hands.

Tech Boy gets up and grabs his hat only for it to dissolve into ash in his hands. That's when he remembers. "That's right. I came face to face with the perpetrator, a being of pure electricity." He stands up and puts his hand to his chin, "But something's not right. He didn't attack until you guys showed up and he never hurt anyone according to him. I don't think he's evil."

Jeremiah scratches his head confused, "Is that possible? How can a villain not be evil?"

"Not everything is black and white. Sometimes people do bad things out of desperation. Evil or not, our objective is clear. We have to chase him out of the plant and restore the power."

"Restore the power? That's it! I have a plan," states Tech Boy.

He whispers it to his teammates and the plan is formed.

Inside a dark room, electricity is crackling from the generator providing the only light source. Robot Boy walks up to the generator alone and a tornado forms around him switching him to his alter-ego, Superhero Smiley Face, a rather tall man with unusually curly hair.

"I know you're in there. Come on out!" demands Superhero Smiley Face as he takes a fighting stance.

Electricity surges through the generator as the electrical humanoid exits and forms in front of it.

"You," states the voice that talked to Tech Boy earlier, "I have no quarrel with you. Leave, now!"

"I wish I could. Unfortunately, you seem to be depriving this planet's people of a valuable resource, so it is my duty to stop you."

"How unfortunate. I'm sorry for what must follow."

His hands shoot lightning electrocuting Superhero Smiley Face. In the room above, Tech Boy runs to the remains of the control panel and takes a look at it placing his hand on it.

"Drat. The panel is too damaged to repair," complains Tech Boy.

"Look over there." Tech Girl points to a circuit breaker behind the generator as lightning flashes from the other side.

"Even if we jumpstart the power, we won't be able to move the crane without the panel," states Tech Boy referring to the crane above and behind the generator.

Tech Girl responds pulling out a little handheld tablet similar to a PDA (Personal Digital Assistant), "You worry about getting the power back on. I'll worry about the crane."

Tech Boy nods perplexed. He launches the grappling hook on the crane and swings to the circuit breakers. SSF narrowly avoids being shocked again. The electrical humanoid retreats into the wires and circles around him. "So what's your name anyway? I don't think I quite caught it."

"Living Static." He rushes out of the wire towards SSF who attempts to block him by taking a defensive stance as his fist is engulfed in flames (Power: Fire Punch). The collision between the fire and electricity creates a small explosion.

The winds storm to Tech Boy's position in front of the circuit breakers. He stands his ground in order to be pushed away by the wind. Once it diminishes, he turns back and continues fiddling with the circuit breaker. "Come on, come on! How much electricity did this guy eat?" The lights spark back to life. Up in the room above, Tech Gril cheers, "Finally." She presses a button on her handheld that now has many wires stuck into a flap on the front of it. The crane springs to life and swings over to the battlefield.

Living Static looks in that direction upon hearing the sound of its movement. He stares at SSF and accuses, "You! You're just a distraction."

SSF admits, "Yes, for phase one of the plan."

The crane stops directly above Living Static.

"However, for phase two!"

The tornado reforms around him putting him close to the safety mark. It dissipates and Jeremiah jumps immediately as Living Static shoots electricity at him. A whip of fire appears in his hand as his watch's alarm starts blaring, the red light blinking in and out. The whip snaps the chain as Living Static hesitates for a brief moment due to the sudden alarm, but a moment is all it takes. The crane falls on him, its impact echoing across the room.

Later, the Superheroes were using a large device similar to a large vacuum cleaner with a clear container attached to it to take Living Static out of the crane and contain him. The boss congratulates, "Good job Sector 17, on another mission."

"Yeah," mumbles Tech Boy looking at Living Static with a downcast look.

He starts walking away, his footsteps audible across the metal floor. Jeremiah looks at him concerned and Tech Girl runs after him, "What's wrong, Tech Boy?" She grabs his shoulder and he stops. Tech Boy turns slightly to look at her.

"It's just…I don't know." He turns around completely training his eyes at the confined Living Static. "I just feel like…there's more to this than we realize."

# **Afterword**

Hello everyone. First of all, I would like to congratulate you all on making it to the end of this anthology/collection, and I hope you'll continue to support me in the future. I'm sure plenty of you have probably figured this out, but this particular collection had a theme going on for it. That theme was Modern Times, especially here in America. I understand that these stories won't be for everyone, and that's fine. I just want to get people thinking about these topics and question why things are happening. You probably got the impression while reading that I'm a bit of a cynic. And that's true. I'm highly cynical. I was going to quote a line from "Checklist" here, but I don't think it would work here. That line was, "I'm practically a genius." The reason why I was thinking of it is because I believe my cynicism comes from my intelligence, allowing me to see some of the problems in the world more easily than others. Sort of like Rick from *Rick and Morty* but without a crippling alcohol addiction and a lot more empathetic. I wonder if that was a good example?

You've probably noticed how I'm using quotation marks for the stories as opposed to italics like I did in the last book. Well, that's very simple to explain. I learned in one of my classes this semester that for citing stories/poems in anthologies/collections, you're supposed to use quotation marks for the specific poem/story while using italics for the collection as a whole, so I'm trying to abide by that rule.

Once again, I would like to thank my brother: Matthew (Matt) Ellison for his excellent cover art. He wanted to make this particular one freeform with an idea he had. I didn't have an idea at the time, so I let him do his thing and here we are. If you want to check out more of his work look up his DeviantArt profile, Ioyity1; his Twitter account, CrystalVerse15; or his Discord user, CrystalizedBean28#5054. I would also like to thank Riley Colins for helping edit "Brain-Washing Vaccine" as his feedback and editing played a minor yet vital role in fleshing out the story of it and inspired me to make the "five years later" portion of it.

Now, I better correct something from the previous Collection's Afterword. You know how I mentioned Grassroots and I thought "The Golden Radiance" was going to be in there? Well, it came out, and I was wrong. The story that did end up in the 2020-2021 issue is "Dark Wizards". Which is still an excellent choice, but everyone tells me that particular story is more of a teaser than anything else. They also want me to make a full-length novel for it, so I would like to know your opinion on it if you had read it. What do you think? Should it become a full-length novel? Let me know your thoughts. If you want to contact me on matters regarding my work, you can contact me at my business email: Jeremiah_Ellison@gmx.com. Now that that has been corrected, let's talk about the actual making of the collection.

The reason why I chose the theme of Modern Times is because I felt these stories needed to be told **now**. Due to how the vast majority of them deal with current events. And I'll admit that one of them is actually non-fiction, but only one: "COVID-19 Saga Past: A World Filled with Fear". This particular story was written when COVID-19 just started as a pandemic and was written for a class assignment. At the time, I never intended for it to resurface, but once I made the speculative fiction piece "COVID-19 Saga Future: The Future" I bundled them together and that was that. Most of these stories I felt needed to come out at this time. Thus, that is why I created Collection 2, to bring them out to the world, for all to see. Now, let's shift gears into *The Superheroes*.

Now *The Superheroes* subsection was actually the toughest portion of the book simply because I had to nearly make everything in it from scratch. The side missions were originally different perspectives of "The Evil Orbs Appear" but while the roughdrafts were all made years ago, I never got around to typing them until I started this collection. Due to the evolution of my writing style the translations were not one-to-one as I always tend to attempt to improve upon the previous iteration. For example, the whole scene where Sector 22 was capturing Icy Pete was practically non-existent in the roughdraft. It was more so Colossal Boy explaining the plan, and then the next sentence stating "The plan was a success" with a very brief and vague description of what each character was doing during that timeframe. That whole chapter just needed an overhaul in general, which these stories were written originally as chapter books. I just converted them to short story format for this collection. "The Wrath of Whirlwind" followed the original roughdraft a little more closely, but the ending entirely changed between the two. Originally, no one died in the roughdraft as opposed to the version in the book where Brawn died. I strongly considered typing up an alternate ending that was more in line with the roughdraft's original ending, but I felt like the new one made a much stronger impact. However, if you would like to read that, let me know. I'm sure it would be a fun time. Plus, I like working with alternate timelines.

Mission 5 was the only story written exclusively for the collection. However, I had a lot of trouble writing it because this is where the series is supposed to start being episodic and as I've been learning while writing, I write serialized stories way better than episodic ones. Something I'm keeping in mind for my latest project, which I can't give details about just yet, but so far has shown promise whenever anyone reads it. Originally, this story was going to be an Evil Orb encounter. But, since the previous two stories in the collection were exactly that, I changed it to introducing the villain Living Static who is supposed to be one of the recurring villains in the series. The horror element in "When Lightning Strikes" comes from the environment. By placing them in a dark power plant with a villain capable of controlling electricity, it really allows me to write a bunch of creative problems/obstacles to overcome. It was originally supposed to be longer but I felt like I hit the points I needed to especially with how Tech Boy was acting throughout the story. One of the primary objectives of this story was to show that the three still need to iron out their teamwork as it wouldn't make much sense if they were able to work as a unit straight from the get-go. I felt like this was achieved in the story and still leaves plenty of room for growth in the characters.

Well, that's about it for this Afterword. I'm not sure when the next Collection is coming out due to school and stuff. However, I do plan on rewriting the stories in *The Superheroes* and selling the missions as eBooks with physical books around every 4 missions or so. That's the plan for now anyway. I hope you enjoy your day, dear reader. Goodbye.

# Bonus Section

# Before We Begin...

Hello everyone, and welcome to the Bonus Section! Before we begin, I would like to state the purpose of this section and how it's going to be handled. Essentially, when we went to publish this book for paperback release way back at the tail end of 2021, Amazon told us no because our spine text was too big. We have tried to fix this many times over the course of the Spring 2022 Semester, but sadly to the same result. We don't know why it's giving us this error in the first place and even when we made the text itty bitty, it still said that the text was too big. Like why? What's the problem? So, we decided to change tactics and toss in this bonus section in order to pad out this book and give my brother more surface area to work with. This section is made some time after the rest of the book was edited and is considered a bit of an addendum to the book with the only changes in the book proper being updated contact information in the Afterword, the addition of the Bonus Section in the Table of Contents, and additional credits on the title page. That's why you saw the Afterword before this section, as that's technically the true ending to the book.

In this section, you will find excerpts of Matthew and I's ongoing/work in progress stories. Naturally because of this, the content is subject to change at a later date. Because the stories in this section can be either by me or my brother, I will put who wrote what at the beginning of each excerpt in order to minimize confusion. Now with that out of the way, I hope you'll enjoy this bonus section.

# Chapter 1: The Dancing Pencil

"Greetings, citizens of Pencilville!" announces a voice in a crowded hall of cheering pencils and pens with thin arms and hands, and of course eyes, but no legs.

"Are you ready to have fun tonight!?"

The crowd cheers even louder.

"Then let's give it up for our star attraction! The Dancing Pencil!"

A lone pencil with a headset hops onto the stage and faces the crowd.

"Hit it!" yells the Dancing Pencil as the music plays. The music itself has got a killer beat with strong bass aided by the reverb the hall provides. The Dancing Pencil begins his dance which consists of a lot of diagonal and angular hopping to the beat. As he dances, the crowd cheers louder. His movements gets faster, and he throws in an occasional flip. The crowd is eating it up. He does a couple of flips and increases his speed for the finale. The Dancing Pencil puts his hand on the floor and goes in circles across the ground as the crowd cheers. Then, he hops back up and ends. The crowd bursts into applause echoing across the hall.

Suddenly, the double doors burst open and in walks two pens, one with his cap on.

"Looks like the Dancing Pen has arrived on the scene. What a shocking turn of events!"

The Dancing Pen hops on stage and says, "Fancy show you got here. I'm impressed."

"Yeah, I bet your ticket sales are as bad as your garbage."

The crowd gasps.

"And isn't that where you're supposed to be? In the garbage?"

Crowd: "Ooooohh!"

"Nah, I argue that where's you should be. I challenge you to a dance-off!"

"A dance-off huh? Remember the last time you faced me?" the Dancing Pen taunts with a smug expression.

"Oh, I did. Which is why I would like to take this opportunity to whoop your eraser."

"You seem to forget I don't have an eraser. I have a base. Either way, bring it on!"

The curtain at the back of the stage draws back revealing a screen which powers on revealing directions similar to that of DDR.

"For those of you unfamiliar with the rules, let me break it down for ya. Our two contestants have to stick as closely to the rhythm as possible and look cool doing it. The more stylish you are, the more points you get. Whoever has the most points by the end of the song wins!"

"You ready?"

"I am. Don't come crying to me on trash day."

Words appear on the screen as a musical prelude sounds, "Ready?"

The contestants get into position eyes on the screen.

"Go!"

The words disappear as solid arrows start scrolling to the empty ones on top of the screen as the music starts playing. They start dancing to the beat following the arrows, music blaring. They were evenly matched at first keeping pace with each other. The Dancing Pen suddenly flips and hits the notes in a semi-spin acquiring more points. The Dancing Pencil speeds up his dancing. He suddenly flips, lands hands-first, and does a break-dance maneuver straight away putting him in the lead.

The Dancing Pen retaliates with a flip, a spin, while speeding up his pace. They go back to basics at breakneck speed using the same angular hops they started with. The crowd cheers. The two contestants look at each other with smug grins. The finale is near, and the notes scroll rapidly on the screen as the music speeds up. The Dancing Pencil jumps high into the air and spins while the Dancing Pen takes full advantage of his cap and spins on his head.

The crowd cheers, "Dancing Pencil! Dancing Pencil!"

"Dancing Pen! Dancing Pen!"

The Dancing Pen hops back up and flawlessly returns to the rhythm. The Dancing Pencil runs, or rather hops rapidly, up the wall. He backflips off of it and nails the landing! No rhythm was lost! The final note plays and everything stops.

A drum roll starts as the spotlights circle around the stage as the announcer announces, "And the winner is…" As the audience waits with bated breath, the spotlight centers on "The Dancing Pencil!"

The crowd erupts into cheer, "Dancing Pencil! Dancing Pencil!"

The Dancing Pen pronounces, "You may have beaten me this time, but next time you won't be so lucky!"

"We'll just have to see about that. I guess next time we'll see you in Penville."

The Dancing Pen storms off-stage in a huff motioning his manager to follow him. They both exit the double doors which close with a slam.

Later at the lobby further in the building full of sideway mattresses known as recliners which act as Pencilville and Penville's equivalent of chairs since pencils and pens can't really bend all that much, they're too rigid, along with a table in the center of it all. The manager is dumping heaps of praise on the Dancing Pencil while counting the cardboard money from tickets sales leaning on a recliner closest to the door.

"Another amazing performance today. You really showed that Dancing Pen who's boss."

"Yeah," mopes the Dancing Pencil on a separate, extra-wide recliner.

"Alright, what's wrong?" asks the manager with target precision.

"It's just…dancing is great and all…"

The manager taps his finger on the table as he says, "Uh-huh."

"And it…pays well, buut don't you think there's more to life than dancing?" philosophizes the Dancing Pencil.

The manager sighs, gets up from leaning on the table, and hops over to the Dancing Pencil. He places his hand on his shoulder where his right arm connects to his wooden body.

"Look, as your manager I'll support any decision you make, just so long as it isn't absolutely insane. However, keep in mind that you have a house to pay for."

He grabs close to half the stack of cash and places it on the table in front of the Dancing Pencil with a thud, "Here is your cut for today."

He goes back and leans on the recliner on the other side of the table. The Dancing Pencil gets up and picks up the money off the table and counts it. Afterwards, he walks out the door and closes it with a thumping sound.

In the urban wasteland known as Penville, the Dancing Pen and his manager are walking back to the Dancing Pen's apartment, sirens blaring in the background.

"And another loss to you, sir," says the manager with a British accent.

The Dancing Pen retorts, "I know that! That big-shot Dancing Pencil thinks he's all that, but without me, he'd be all washed up."

"Your rent for your apartment is coming soon. What do you plan to do about it?"

"That pickshole? Barely qualifies as a living quarters. Luckily, I got a plan," he says looking at the Penville 1st National Bank.

It was a peaceful day in Pencilville. The sun was shining ever so brightly down on the surface of Object World. Winged erasers chirping in the background. The wind blowing a gentle breeze. It was a beautiful day in Pencilville, yet the Dancing Pencil, now out of his stage attire with backpack in tow, trudges through the street with a sullen look conflicted about his future.

The tranquility is shattered by the sudden outburst of a bank alarm, right before a fiery, booming burst of flames explodes out of the front entrance of the brick building known as the Pencilville 1st National Bank. As smoke rises out of the new hole in the bank's front entrance, five indistinguishable shadows rush out of the bank holding mostly spherical objects.

"Come on, let's get out of here!" yells one of the shapes.

They run deeper into the black smoke. Police sirens could be heard in the distance. The Dancing Pencil's sullen looks change to those of fierce determination. He casts aside his backpack landing on the ground with a soft thump before rushing tiplong into the rising smoke.

The thieves stop at the crosswalk looking frantically. "Which way was the hideout again?"

"Stop right there you thieves!"

They look in the direction the voice came from as the Dancing Pencil dashes out of the smoke tackling the nearest robber down to the ground with a great big thump. Sirens draw closer. One robber kicks the Dancing Pencil with his eraser with great impact rolling him off the other one. He helps his teammate up as the Dancing

Pencil jumps back to his eraser. "We don't have time for this!" The robber closest to the crosswalk who just yelled that pulls out a blaster and starts shooting. As if an internal rhythm starts playing in his tip, he starts dancing to avoid the lasers. Left. Right. Left. Right. Forward Flip. The Dancing Pencil lands on the shooter's tip and literally dances him, down to the ground. In a rhythm similar to tap dancing, he uses his own weight to stomp him down to the concrete pavement of the sidewalk. Angered by his actions, another robber rushes in for a punch, but is outright denied as the Dancing Pencil pirouettes out of the way and sweeps him knocking him down to the ground. The remaining two tackle him with a thud pinning him down to the ground when the police sirens close in.

"Drat! We're out of time! Get your loot and go!"

The other robbers get up and grab their loot. However, as they attempt to escape, several police cars screech to a stop right in front of them and surround them from every direction coating the area in odd hue of red and blue light as the sirens reach a fever pitch. A multitude of cops flock out of the cars and aim their blasters at them.

One officer grabs a megaphone and orders, "Freeze! You're all under arrest!

They are promptly handcuffed with a loud clank.

Back in Penville, the Dancing Pen is laughing manically in an alley as smoke rises from the Penville 1st National Bank. He hops away, sacks of cash in hand, as the police drive by, sirens in the background.

Back in Pencilville as the robbers were being loaded up into cars on the darkened street now full of blue and red light, one of them warns rather loudly, "We'll remember this! You better watch out because one day we will have our revenge!" The door closes with a loud thump and click. A few officers load up into their cars and drive away. One officer approaches the Dancing Pencil and says, "We'll need you to come with us." "Right," he says to the officer before hopping into the pitch-black inside of the car.

The next day, the manager slams down the latest newscarboard on the table with the headline "Dancing Pencil thwarts Bank Robbery" as the manager scolds him, "What were you THINKING!? You could have gotten yourself killed!"

He stutters, "I was just…I just…I wanted to help. It was so sudden, I just…leapt into action."

"Good publicity or not," he begins as he tosses the Dancing Pencil's discarded backpack on the table where it lands with a thud, "Never do something like that again. A dead client is no good to me!"

"Yes sir!" quickly salutes the Dancing Pencil scared for his own life.

"Good. Now excuse me while I go capitalize on your recent blunder." The manager grabs a flip phone and starts making some calls.

In the city of Penville, the Dancing Pen is staring out of the window gazing upon the desolate surroundings, smog rising up from a chemical plant, as he leans upon a sack of stolen money. The door opens with a squeak and his manager's steps could be heard coming towards him.

"Sir, I have something you'll want to see," says the manager as he presents the latest newscarboard to him. The Dancing Pen turns around and takes a look at the front page headline "Dancing Pencil thwarts Bank Robbery". He mumbles to himself, "That waste of pencil shavings."

"What do you want to do sir?"

He tosses the newscarboard at the manager's head and he says, "Leave it. It will do us no good at this moment to intervene. Now go do your job! This publicity is sickening me."

The newscarboard falls on the floor as the manager simply says, "Yes sir," before leaving. Once he left, the Dancing Pen picks up the newscarboard once more and spies a picture of the robbers and he muses, "I wonder."

Back at Pencilville, the Dancing Pencil is being blinded by the flashing lights of the press over at the hastily assembled outdoor press conference in Pencilville square. The Dancing Pencil is behind a large podium with several microphones stationed on top and small stairs on the back of it.

"How did it feel taking on those bank robbers?" asks a reporter.

"Well, it was kind of scary, but exhilarating at the same time."

"What compelled you to take them on?" asks another reporter.

"I just felt like I needed to do something."

"Are you part of a rival gang, and if so, was this a war over territory?"

"What?"

The sheer surprise and absurdity of that question left the Dancing Pencil speechless. The manager stepped in and says, "No further questions. This conference is over." Of course, this didn't stop the frenzy of reporters from asking anyway as the manager led the Dancing Pencil away to his car shielding him from the mob. They hop into the car and drive away.

"Hopefully, leaving at that specific question doesn't create any negative publicity. Of course, I better keep an eye on those tabloids," says the manager beating around the bush.

"I don't know what happened. That question was so out of the blue that I froze. I wasn't mentally prepared for it," explains the Dancing Pencil.

"Neither was I. I had a feeling that if that conference kept going, it would have went downhill fast. I was not ready nor willing to take that bet."

They arrive at the Dancing Pencil's small house in the suburbs. After opening the car doors and closing them creating a clicking sound. They hop over to the house and the Dancing Pencil sticks his key into the keyhole on the front door and turns it until he hears the clicking sound indicating the door is unlocked. He puts the key away and opens the door with its squealing hinges. The inside of the house was pitch black. The manager hops inside as the Dancing Pencil fumbles for the light switch. He finds it and flicks the switch filling the room with light. The Dancing Pencil offers, "Have a recliner." The manager takes him on the offer and leans on the recliner. He sighs in relief. The Dancing Pencil hops over to the kitchen and asks, "Can I get you anything?"

"Water, please." The Dancing Pencil takes out a couple of glasses out of his cupboard and fills them up in the sink. One is filled and he places it on the counter making a little clinking noise as he fills the other one. Once it's full, he turns the water off and takes the glasses to the table. He sets them down on the table and hops over to his other recliner.

"Ahh," breathes the Dancing Pencil.

The manager grabs his cup of water, goes back to leaning on the recliner, and takes a sip of his water. "Ahh. Delicious," comments the manager in a tranquil tone of voice. A knock sounds from the door and reverberates through the room. The manager gets up and looks at the door.

"Are you expecting anyone?"

"No."

The knocks get louder. The manager and the Dancing Pencil look at each other and back at the door. The Dancing Pencil gets up and approaches the door slowly. Suddenly, it bursts open revealing the robbers from earlier.

"I told you we'd be back."

They start blasting and the Dancing Pencil barely dances out of the way while the manager hides behind his recliner. The Dancing Pencil quickly jumps behind the same recliner. Laser fire hits the wall leaving scorch marks on it making loud bangs. They concentrate their fire on the recliner but some of it still misses and hits the wall. The manager panics, "What are we going to do? We're completely defenseless!"

"That's not entirely true, but my blaster is behind the other recliner."

They look at the other recliner and the manager is stunned. However, he breathes deeply. He says, "I got a crazy idea. I can't believe that I'm going to suggest this but…" He whispers the rest to the Dancing Pencil who nods in agreement. They push their current recliner at the robbers, and it hits them knocking them down. The manager quickly hops over to the other one going around the table while the Dancing Pencil hops on the table and quickly slides under there from the other side. The robbers struggle under the weight of the first recliner, but they are able to barely push it off of them causing it to land on the floor face-down. They get back up and continue blasting leaving more scorch marks on the walls. The Dancing Pencil slides open a secret compartment in the back of his chair revealing an odd blaster made of stone with strange markings/characters on it.

"That's your weapon? That thing looks like it belongs in a museum."

"Yeah, I…umm…made it myself with stuff I found on the street."

One of the blasts hit a little too close to home reminding them of the grave danger they're in as the enemy concentrates fire on the second recliner to their best degree, and the recliner is starting to burn away. They nod at each other, but the manager is obviously still in a panic. The Dancing Pencil leans out of cover and shoots a robber knocking him down. The other four concentrate their fire on him and the Dancing Pencil barely gets back under cover. He climbs above the recliner and shoots at the robber in the back who shoots back at him. The lasers collide and coalesce into a strange cloud.

"What the-"

Before they could finish that sentence, the cloud bursts into six lasers that hit everyone but the manager knocking the Dancing Pencil down to the floor knocking everyone out. The manager starts shaking the Dancing Pencil while panicking, "Hey, are you ok? Wake up. WAKE UP!"

# Chapter 2: Pencilman

The sound of a heart monitor echoes throughout the sterilized white room. The Dancing Pencil is lying down on a white hospital bed with blue blankets. His manager is leaning down on a very small recliner, that is more like a suspended pillow than a whole mattress, next to his bed, racked with worry.

Suddenly, a groan could be heard from the Dancing Pencil. He slowly opens his eyes as the dark void of his vision is suddenly filled with the lights of the hospital room.

"Where am I?" asks the dazed pencil.

"The hospital," replies the manager.

"How did I get here?" asks the Dancing Pencil groggily.

"You were attacked by those thugs you thwarted the other day."

He rises up and groans, "Oh."

Then, it hits him. "Wait a minute. Why did they get out of jail so fast? It makes no sense." As he holds his hands to his tip panicking, he starts floating up. The manager quickly hops up knocking the recliner back a bit and stares at the Dancing Pencil, his mouth wide open in disbelief.

"How are you floating!?" blurts out the manager.

That question hits him like a truck, and he looks down noticing the blanket now down on the floor and notices that his entire body is off the ground. He starts screaming and panicking as his entire body shifts in every possible direction among the 3 axes.

"Whoa! What is going on?"

The manager, his voice cracking, moves his hands downwards as he says, "Calmm down. Just, gently, float down." The Dancing Pencil stops in midair and takes a deep breath and slowly descends until he's finally, safely on the floor. The manager helps him up and asks confused and worried, "So, umm…how did you do that?"

"I don't know," replies the Dancing Pencil shaking his tip.

Suddenly, they hear basesteps in the hallway. The door opens with a squeal and the doctor hops in.

"Good to see you're awake," says the doctor upon entering. She closes the door and says, "According to your test results, the damage you've sustained is minimal. However, I'll need to do additional tests just to be sure."

The Dancing Pencil gulps and mutters, "Ok."

He is seated on the bed as the doctor gets out a small stone hammer and hits him with it causing him to yell in pain and kick upward sending his whole body in the air, where it remains for a few seconds.

"Another case," mumbles the doctor before the Dancing Pencil crashes into the bed breaking it in two.

"Another case?" questions the manager firmly in shock.

"Sorry, I'm not allowed to divulge any other information than that. We'll need to keep him overnight for observation," states the doctor.

The manager says in concern, "I don't like the sound of that."

"Don't worry. If anything happens, we'll contact you immediately. We just need your phone number."

She hands him the clipboard with a piece of cardboard on it. He attaches it to the wall using the magnet on the other side of the clipboard and uses his tip to write down the necessary information. Afterwards, he takes it off the wall and hands it to the doctor.

"Thank you. If anything happens, we'll be sure to let you know."

"Alright, then. Mark, I'll check up on you first thing in the morning. Don't cause the doctors too much trouble," states the manager as he hops to the door.

"Geez. You sound like my father," says the Dancing Pencil.

He turns around and replies, "I'm not, but I'm the guy who gives you your rent money so you might want to listen to me."

The manager opens the squealing door and hops out the room as the Dancing Pencil shakes his tip in amusement.

The night itself was relatively peaceful except for the constant screaming in the back of the hospital making it relatively hard for the Dancing Pencil to sleep. Somehow, he finds a way and drifts off to sleep.

The next day, he is released from the hospital. They hop inside the manager's car, close the doors, and the manager places his eraser on the green go button allowing the car to drive off. It doesn't take long to get to the stadium Mark performed in yesterday. Once they're inside the lobby, they plop down on separate recliners exhausted from the craziness of yesterday.

"So, superpowers, huh?" asks the manager.

"Yeah," replies Mark.

Silence.

"You still have them?"

"Yeah," replies Mark.

More silence.

"Can you show me?" asks the manager.

"Sure," replies Mark.

He gets off the recliner and hops over to the side. The manager gets up himself to have a better view. Once he was also on the side, Mark starts concentrating closing his eyes as he floats off the ground.

"Holy aluminum."

Mark opens up his eyes and yells, "Holy aluminum, I'm flying!"

The manager exclaims, "You were the one who told me you could do it!"

"Well, yeah, but I didn't think I actually could."

The manager sighs in disbelief shaking his tip with his hands at his tip border.

"So now what? You got these awesome powers. What are you going to do with them?"

The Dancing Pencil, still in the air, closes his eyes and starts pondering this. He opens them as an idea pops in his head sounding like a mental "ding".

"Oh, I got an idea. What if I become a superhero and stop all the crime in Pencilville?" suggests the Dancing Pencil.

"You're joking, right? May I remind you how you ended up in the hospital in the first place?" reminds the manager.

"Yeah, I know. But…"

"No! No buts. Absolutely no buts."

"Just hear me out."

"No."

"But-"

"What did I just say!?"

"No buts."

"Exactly."

"But…"

"Stop it!"

"With these powers…"

"I said stop."

"I would have a much better chance of succeeding."

"Dang it Mark! Ok, I'll hear you out."

Mark explains, "When I faced those robbers last time, there was no sign or clue that I even had these abilities. But now, I can suddenly fly and with a little practice; I feel like I can make a difference."

The manager sighs, "If we do this thing, we have to keep your identity a secret. We can't have supervillains attack your concerts and take your audience hostage or something like that."

"Of course," replies Mark.

They immediately got to work. The first thing they decided to work on was the costume. So, they went to the clothing store, which in Object World is a very niche market, to buy some clothes. When they walk in the store sounding a little bell, the manager of the store manning the counter yells out in joy, "Finally! Now I won't have to declare bankruptcy!"

This caught them off guard as they look at the store manager with pained expressions before deciding just to move on and buy some clothes.

The first outfit they try on is a big black trench coat and sunglasses. The manager shakes his head, "Gives off the wrong kind of vibe."

Next, they go for a trashy, outdated hipster look with an oversized pink shirt and baggy one-legged pants. The manager grimaces in disgust and comments, "Now that one is just plain ugly."

His third choice was a rock-star ensemble complete with a leather jacket, sunglasses, and a fake head of hair. The manager puts his hand to his tip and shakes it in disbelief. "You're as popular, but you're not a rock star. You're more of a pop sensation." Mark shoots a "Really?" look at him to which the manager simply says, "What?" He closes the curtain.

A few minutes later, Mark opens the curtain and the manager's face sinks.

"A cape, seriously?"

"I like it," says Mark doing a twirl.

"Well, it's better than your other choices."

The cash register rings as they purchase the cape as the manager of the store begs, "Are you sure you don't want to buy anything else? I can offer a great deal on tuxedos." The manager replies, "I'm sure," before leaving the store.

…

Back at the dance studio's lounge, Mark and his manager are leaning on recliners. Mark says, "Next up, we need a name for my superhero identity. I'm thinking Pencilman. What do you think?"

The manager replies, "Sounds kind of basic, but it'll do." He gets up from his recliner and asks, "Anything else we need to take care of, aside from practice of course?"

Mark gets up and puts his hands below his face as he thinks for a moment. He responds, "Yeah, there's one more thing. I need a sidekick."

The manager exclaims, "And where the lead are you going to find one?"

He hops to the wall behind him as he states, "I don't know. But…"

The manager hops on over there as Mark starts drawing on the wall with his tip. "I need someone who is strong and agile, with a quick wit about him, and maybe a little flexible, like so." Mark finishes drawing a piece of paper with a face of determination making a fist with one of the corners stretching out.

The manager comments, "They really taught you well in art school."

Mark nods and agrees before the manager continues, "You do realize the paper people are extinct-"

The drawing suddenly turns white as the hand retracts. The drawing uses its corners to push itself off the wall and lands the floor making a crunkling sound. As Mark and the manager stare at the living piece of paper in silence, it asks bending his upper corners creating another crumpling sound, "Who am I?"

The manager attempts to vocalize, "You…brought back…a paper person? How?"

Mark says, "My drawings come to life. Cool."

He hops over to the paper person and says, "Hello, my name is Mark and I brought you to life."

The manager looks at him like he's crazy.

"For now, we're going to call you Paperboy and I want you to be my sidekick."

"Sidekick?"

"It means I want you to help me fight crime."

Paperboy thinks about this for a moment and happily nods. Suddenly, the TV comes on.

"This is an urgent news bulletin. A gang of thugs has decided to rob a jewelry store and is currently making their getaway. All citizens are advised to remain indoors as the police try to apprehend them."

Mark says, "Time to get to work."

Mark grabs his cape and ties it around his "neck", the point where his tip meets the rest of him. A ring appears around Paperboy. It splits into two with one ascending his body while the other descends it. In the area the ring crosses, a cape appears on his back transforming him into his superhero outfit.

Mark questions, "How did you do that?"

"I don't know," answers Paperboy.

"Whatever," says Mark as he slams open the window. He jumps out of it creating a huge gust of wind knocking down the manager as he flies out the window. Paperboy follows him by jumping and flying out the window as well.

They fly at breakneck speeds through the city of Pencilville swerving from building to building until they arrive at the crime scene. They look down and see the perpetrators fleeing. Pencilman crashes down into the ground right in front of his; his impact creating a huge crater in the street. Sadly, he is not invulnerable as pain fills out his entire body as he thinks to himself, "I hope I won't need duct tape after this." Paperboy lands right behind him to his left inside the crater.

One of the thugs asks, "Who are you?"

He gets up ignoring the pain and turns to face the robbers boldly staring at them dead in the eye as he declares, "I am Pencilman!"

Paperboy chimes in, "And I'm his sidekick Paperboy!"

"And we are here to take you down!" finishes Pencilman.

"Ahh! Necromancer! He brought a paper person back to life!" yells one of them as he starts running.

The other two chase after him screaming for him to come back. They both just look as the scene in disbelief as Pencilman states, "I hope that won't be a common occurrence."

"What did he mean by necromancer?" asks the naïve Paperboy.

"I'll tell you later," states Pencilman.

The thugs are running to the side, the one in front screaming, "I don't wannna die! I don't wanna die!"

"Get back here you moron. You still have the jewels!"

He tosses the jewels back at his partner as he hops away screaming. Pencilman takes off creating huge wind pressure in the crater, but he overshoots his targets and crashes into a nearby building causing it to start collapsing. People start screaming both inside and outside the building scared of their impending demise. The robbers run away from the scene only to be blocked by the police who just arrived on the scene flooding red and blue light on them. Paperboy flies over and stretches his entire body to catch the building before it totally collapses.

Pencilman gets back up from behind the building and rubs his tip. He looks over and sees Paperboy doing his best to slow the building's collapse.

"I didn't realize you could stretch that far."

"Neither did I."

Many pencils start climbing out the windows of the building. Not all were unscathed though. Some were cracked. Some were broken in two and being dragged out by their friends and family. One came out holding a roll of duct tape as big as their bodies.

Pencilman, seeing the robbers apprehended and police looking up at the scene, says, "I'm going to look for more stragglers."

Before Paperboy could say anything, Pencilman takes off and crashes into the wall making a new hole in it. He stands up and rubs his newly cracked tip. Pencilman runs around the hallways looking inside the rooms of the building for stragglers. He spots a couple of young pencils, significantly taller than him trying to hide behind some recliners. Pencilman runs over to them, but they cower away from him.

He holds out his hand says, "I'm here to help."

They stay silent not daring to move.

Pencilman looks around him and spots a nearby wall. He runs to it, hoping his hunch is correct. He nervously, but swiftly, draws a door on the wall. The drawing changes color to a more wooden brown as a doorknob pops out. The kids throw all caution to the wind and jump out the door, bouncing safely on Paperboy. Pencilman tries flying again, but crashes into the wall cracking his midriff. He gets back up rubbing his midriff as a pencil slightly younger than him runs over to him and shakes him while asking frantically, "Yo, are you the guy who made the door?"

He responds, "Yeah, do you need help?"

"Oh, thank creator, yes! My entire family is stuck behind some rubble, and I need to save them."

"Lead the way."

They run to the guy's apartment. Inside, there is a whole heap of rubble smack dab in the middle of the room. Pencilman has no clue where to start. All of a sudden, the building shakes as the windows open and paper hands come through. The giant paper hands grab chunks of the debris and drag it outside.

Pencilman looks up and sees a small gap at the top of the rubble giving him an idea. As Paperboy grabs more rubble, Pencilman takes off slowly and carefully draws a huge door on the wall making sure it overlays the area of debris. Drawing the dividing line on the other side past the rubble, he finishes up the other side of the drawing which turns into a huge gray door. He kicks it open on his current side as the other guy opens the other side. Gravity does its work spewing gravel like a waterfall while Paperboy feels the pain of the impact.

"Ow, ow, ow."

Pencilman flies in front of the family and grabs them. He flies out of there at decent speed prioritizing control over speed.

He lands safely as the rubble waterfall subsides. Letting go of the family, Pencilman flies back inside slowly, grabs the man, and flies back out. Paperboy finally returns to normal size finally allowing the building to fall; the impact unleashing a thunderous roar that echoes across the city.

Pencilman looks around and sees the robbers inside the police cars and breathes a sigh of relief. However, somebody taps on his shoulder and he turns around, only to be met with a cardboard bill.

"In light of your heroism, I will not press charges for the destruction of the building provided you pay for the damages," states the landlord holding the bill.

Pencilman awkwardly takes the bill and yammers, "Umm…sure. Can we talk about an installment plan?"

The landlord motions for them to follow him and they comply.

Back at the hospital, a scream burst forth from behind the double doors of a room in the Emergency Ward where the bank robbers that tried to kill Pencilman lie; only nothing is right. One is constantly bursting into flames; another one is in a constant state of melting, his body contorting in unnatural ways as he drowns in himself; a third struggling against his constraints as bursts of wind spiral forth from his being; the fourth with the floor coated in ice; and the fifth struggling with movement so rapid that it's inconceivable. The doctors and nurses are scrambling just to keep them stable. A group of them is blown away by the windy one hitting the equipment, albeit not that hard.

"I need 50ml of sedative, stat."

One such nurse approaches with weighted clothes and grabs the thing of anesthesia. Loud thumps could be heard as she approaches the screaming patient. Another gust of wind blows, but she remains in place. She injects the anesthesia, and he falls asleep. The fire guy screams as he is lit ablaze as the foaming stream of a fire extinguisher douses him, and that's the 5th one they had to use that day. They attempt to approach him but he ignites again, panics, and shoots a blast of fire from his restrained palm. Everyone in the line of fire jumps out of the way as the blast hits the wall scorching it.

The ice guy is the easiest to deal with as long as they don't stand still long enough to completely freeze over, constantly breaking the ice off that forms around them off their erasers. The speedy one is tough to hold down even with the restraints, but with at least 5-6 different nurses holding him down, they can work on him.

The toughest challenge of all is the guy constantly melting, his screams echoing across the room. Several "limbs" constantly rise up out of his body only to sink back down as if he's constantly drowning within himself. The doctor rushes over and takes another sample using a syringe as the nurses stand back watching in terror. He observes the sample's DNA, but shakes his tip at the lack of information it provides.  They look at their patients in horror and worry as the speedy one knocks off another bolt in his restraint.

# **<u>Identity Crisis</u>** *by Matthew Ellison*

# **Warning**

These are set in First Person POV.

All characters that are not owned by me, Ioyity/Pokematt, do belong to their respective owners and I do not claim ownership in any way, shape, or form.

These books are in the same style as LDA's (Lyric's Dimensional Adventure) "End of Section" Chapters, but heavily toned up with the lore.

Lyric Hunton, Ioy, or any other original characters that may appear in this lore are owned by their respective owners, which will be me most of the time.

A Megalo Stream, Identity Crisis, and other lores that will overlap will happen when the events in the lores meet, chronologically.

In this regard, please do not think that I have stolen ideas from anyone, as any and all characters in this that are mine were made from scratch and from my own mind.

Please note that some lore books may contain gore, strong language, graphic imagery, mature themes, depression related problems, self-harm, and/or sexual imagery. If you do not want to read those, or just hate those, then read with caution. And note that if anything includes sexual themes and/or imagery, that all characters when said events happened are either at or above age of 18.

Ioy's Age does change a lot in this.

Along with this, this sneak peak only goes up to chapter 3, "Endeavors Into New Beginnings." I haven't really had motivation to really crack down and write the rest of the story like Jeremiah has, but I do have the book planned out, but I'll be doing short stories based on my vision on this.

The story has been formatted to fit this collection with a touch of how it'll look in the book it'll be derived from, so if you do enjoy what you read and wanna chat about it, I will leave my socials below!

Please enjoy!

Socials:

Deviantart: Ioyity

Twitter: CrystalVerse15

Discord: CorVoid28#2959

# A "NORMAL" LIFE

## *AGES 0-8*

What seemed to be a normal life, turned out to be not so normal. I was born into a family of full blooded Nekcons (Cat-Human Hybrids; Hated by Humans) but was brought to a human family because of my parent's death. For whatever reason, they accepted me in, even though I had Nekcon ears and a tail. I'm not so sure they even knew what a Nekcon was at the time, but it was certainly something that they even bothered to take me in.

For the first few 7 years of my life, I had to hide my identity as a Nekcon. I was bullied by everyone about my appearance. About how I shouldn't've even mattered in the first place, how I should not even be cared for because I was a Nekcon. My parents quickly found out about this and did their own research about my race, Nekcons, and how they were in a massive Nekcon-Human War and that Nekcons are basically hated by most humans. They soon quickly learned how Nekcons could use magic, with the easiest spell to learn being to hide their ears and tail. I soon learned that, after many failed attempts because of my undeveloped magic, I hid my ears and tail from everyone that was outside of my household. I was ashamed of my identity. It was like I never even mattered in the end anymore, I felt like shit for so long that I eventually attempted suicide. I was found while hanging mid-air, and was rushed to the hospital, still hiding my Nekcon ears and tail, I was diagnosed with severe depression, given medication to help with it, and was sent home. I just sat down in my room on my bed the rest of the night doing nothing but think less of myself. I barely got any sleep for the upcoming nights.

# A DOWNWARD SPIRAL



Aug 14, 2012, my 9th birthday. I feel incredibly sleepy, but I have not been able to sleep one bit. I do not understand why myself but all I know currently, is that I do not want to have this day happen at all, it reminds me of how much of a freak I really am. It does not matter if anyone says I'm not a freak, it doesn't even matter what they think of me.

## I. AM. A. MONSTER.

They all say that I am perfectly fine the way I am. But, how can I? All my life I have had people just look at me and say how much I am "one of those." All I want to do is stay in bed, the whole day, just in bed. But I will not, I will be strong about this and let this day happen because of the people that care about me. They want me to have a good time today. So, for today only, I will pretend to have a good time when its not what I want. I hide my issues from my "family" because I do not want them to worry about me at all. Why bother caring about a freak? You do not. You want them dead, burnt, and anything else that can happen to them. Everything that has led up to this moment was just a waste of time, and a waste of my energy. That is not a good thing however, as I have let them in on my issues by accident.

It is 12:43 pm, everyone but me is eating. I am in my room looking at the ceiling while thinking to myself. For once in my life I unhide my ears and tail and lay down.

"Why must this day happen? Its pointless. I'm just a freak and that's never going to change." I say as I curl up into a ball with my tail curling with me and covering part of me while my ears go down. (Note: Ears going down means a sign of depression/sad feelings in this universe.) I then hear a scream that makes me jump, conceal my Nekcon identity, and get off the bed as I turn to the door and see a woman staring at me through the door.

"Oh. My. God. He is a fucking freak! Why is he here?! Hey kid, maybe you should go back to where you came from and never be here again!" She said while tapping her foot. My mother came by and basically dragged her out of the room, slammed the door shut and was yelling at her, though muffled, I could make out what she was saying. She was yelling at her about making me feel so shitty about myself and that she should be ashamed of herself because of my depression. All while I go lay back down on my bed and curl back up. I'm left feeling so shitty about myself that all that's on my mind is the words, on loop, "I. Am. A. Monster."

For the next few days, I feel incredibly depressed to the point that nothing seems to matter to me and I just sit in all my classes not doing anything 'till my parents get called to the office from home, and I'm pulled out from class and into the office as well and the topic of this trip is how I've felt for the past few days. I haven't been working on any of the assignments, haven't done any notes, it just seems that I have stopped caring about school altogether. But unfortunately, it goes much worse than that, as I've stopped caring about life. My parents start thinking of putting me into therapy because later that day I tried another attempt at suicide, only this time, with a knife to my heart. I was rushed to the ER and had to be placed under life-supports to keep me alive while I heal. My heart had stopped and for a while I couldn't move my body at all. I eventually recovered to where I could move again but I really didn't like that as all I wanted to do was escape this world and all that it contained. Nothing made sense as to why I was still alive in the first place. As far as I knew, I was a monster and a freak that shouldn't deserve anything of what I had to begin with. Was it all a lie? Did I deserve everything I had?

A year later and I'm now in therapy. Its going great actually, I'm starting to feel like that maybe I do deserve what I have. And for all my life I've always thought that people with a tail and cat ears were casted out, not to be mentioned ever. But now I'm starting to rethink that this is actually false, and that people are just idiots and refuse to let me have my own freedom because of how I really am. While knowing that I may not be as much as a freak as I really am, I still don't really want to come out as my true identity. To me, nothing makes any sense; if its ok for me to be who I really am, then why don't people accept me for who I am?  What did I do to them to make them not accept me? I can no longer tell anything. Nothing is making any sense anymore. Why do I exist now? Just to suffer? Just to be picked on? I don't know anymore. I want to know but I also don't want to know either. It all just starts to hurt again the more I think about it. Why does it hurt? Is this normal? Am I supposed to hurt this bad? It's all confusing to me. Maybe it just takes a bit of time.

For the next two years, things start to fit more than they did than when I was 10. I'm starting to understand it a lot more and feel less of a freak and more like I could fit in. It's starting to hurt less now and I think that's only because I'm getting older. I start doing better in school, paying attention, and getting help when I need it. Everyone at my school is so understanding with me and how I can have a mental breakdown at random points because of my depression, they'll be here for me and comfort me when I'm crying myself out. I don't know what I did for them to do this but I love it. I've never had so much people who are actually being nice to me. It feels nice. While breaking down doesn't feel as nice, I get cheered up pretty fast because I'm not used to being treated so nice by anyone other than my family. Now-a-days it hurts to be near anyone outside my circle of friends, school staff and my family. Most people will refuse to treat me like an actual human being. It really just brings me down into depression more, but I can get healed pretty fast because of the therapy sessions.

Grade School Graduation Day came by, and I was slightly excited but also didn't want this to happen what-so-ever. It was one of those days where I didn't want to do anything but stare off into space and do nothing else. So, I wake up and instantly realize what day it is. I get up so my family thinks that I'm fine and get ready for the day. I put my gown and cap on and with my family, we go out to my town's community center for the graduation. The graduation goes as expected, my ears and tail are still hidden and that's all that matters…. right? After the graduation, my family and I all go to Dairy Queen to celebrate. As I have been doing all day this morning, I'm simply acting like I'm ok and that nothing is wrong with me today, when in reality, all I wanna do is just go home and stare at the ceiling and hope that this day never even happened. Nothing about me should ever matter right? That's how I see it anyway. I'm just a nobody who should be dead. I really don't see why people would want me to be alive now, all I am is a freak, stupid, and a bunch of other things people call me. It just doesn't seem like anyone wants me around anymore.

# ENDEAVORS INTO NEW BEGINNINGS

*AGE 13*

It's time for high school, I just spent the entire summer before this time just staring at the ceiling of my room, apart from the camping trip mid-summer anyway. The first few days of this "adventure" as people are calling it for whatever reason even though it really isn't one, are okay-ish. They're not anything special but I guess I can't determine what is special or not seeming as I, myself, am special but think that I am a monster anyway. Only thing that seems to happen so far in this is that people are more accepting to me for who I really am, I'm actually making some friends here and there and even though its not much, I'd still say that this is a better life right now than it was at the start of grade school; but at the same time it's just a waste of time. Why waste your time hanging out with people who are more likely to "care" about you? It seems that they will just leave you behind at some point or another and won't notice it at all. They will keep living this live without you till you step in and point it out. Its why I don't like making any friends what-so-ever, because in the end they will betray you in some way or another and I know for a fact it will hurt. It always will hurt, no matter who it is and no matter where it is. Because all I'm meant to be is a freak, a nobody. I shouldn't be cared for, I don't deserve to be cared for. I just want to die! Why won't it come to me?! Why can't I see the light? Is there no light at all? What if I'm not good enough to see the light. What if I'm supposed to suffer everyday for the rest of my life, knowing I'll never find love, find friends, find anyone. I'll suffer all alone and nobody would care at all. I'm getting off topic here. Freshman year wasn't that bad, but it was filled with depression and such. I often found myself just not paying attention to anything and end up nearly breaking down, though I was sent to the office when that happens and their trying to help me move on from the past. But it's simply not the past that's the reasoning why I'm breaking down so much, it's simply me feeling like I shouldn't be here and how I shouldn't even exist at all.

I have little voices in my head at times that yell out "you shouldn't exist", or "you're a freak and everyone wants you gone." It's just the depression talking though, but it still hurts to hear that, you know? I hear those words everyday of my life, at the same times, during the same class. Always:

## "*YOU. DON'T. MATTER.*"

But I suppose it wasn't all bad… right? Well, sometime into my Freshman year of high school, I met an odd fellow that I created back in 2014, Lyric Hunton. He would be the reason everything changes. I can't say enough about how much change he's done to my life by meeting me. And, it was hard to believe that it was really him. I didn't believe it was him the first time, I thought that no character that anyone makes up, couldn't come to life, but here was one. A character that I made, come to life, and having all his backstory already happened. He gave me his jacket as a way of trying to help me with my depression, saying that I could just think of the one person that will never say "you're a freak," Him. He's the one person that will forever believe I can achieve what I want to do without any trouble. That I can get past my depression, get past everything that's been told to me, that I have support. But it still felt…wrong, that he really isn't real, that I'm just imagining him being here. But it's all real. He's truly standing right in front of me, jacket at hand, ready to hand it over to me. I'm a bit hesitate to take it, but I eventually take it, and he makes a copy of it, hands the copy to me and puts the other one on and flies off. I say thank you to him and starts walking in the school. Going back in the school doesn't really feel all that great. It just feels like a hellish prison. 'It's just something I have to deal with.' That's just something I tell myself to keep myself from running away completely. Because effectively, I need the education anyway, and running away now before I get it? Be a waste of time don't you agree? With the jacket at hand now, it feels like my life is just more fights rather than anything else. Only reason it feels like it's more fights, is just simply cause I can't go a few minutes without being attacked. But what ended up to be fun for the first few minutes, soon became my eventual downfall deeper in my hole.

It's been a couple of months since I've had this jacket, and I've learned how to use all of it's abilities so far, but while doing school work, time was frozen, which is what happens when danger is detected nearby as per instructions of the jacket given by Lyric himself. I head towards the danger and soon found out that it was just a worm monster thing. I quickly evacuated everyone that was in the gym so nobody else got hurt. How ironic that was since after one blast using every ability I had access to, unfortunately it was repelled at me after striking the monster. I got hit right in the heart. Hearing my friends call out for me, the monster explodes. Being knocked backwards, I fall onto the floor, unable to move my body, and eventually turning into dust, something I can't even explain.

All I see is a void. An empty, black, void.

# <u>A Former Superhero</u> *by Jeremiah and Matthew Ellison*

## Chapter 1: A Former Hero Meets An Agency

In an abandoned warehouse in the outskirts of some town a door opens and a guy with ruby red eyes, brown hair, and a slightly average yet partially bulky build flies out the door clinging on to several flyers before falling down back down to the ground on his butt. (Jeremiah Ellison, Series: The Superheroes, Author: Jeremiah) The door slams shut. He gets up and dusts himself off. As he goes to retrieve the flyers on the ground he mumbles to himself grouchily, "Dang Alucard, sending me here to advertise. Was kicking me in the rear really necessary? I missed the old days when I had that solid gold castle. Oh well, next time I'll read the fine print when I apply for a job." He finished picking up the flyers and started heading to town. While he heads to town, he spots a giant monster attacking that town while also being attacked by two floating guys, one seems to be aiming an arrow at that big monster and the other seems to be glowing up a Random-Ass-Sword Sword.

"HEY FUCKER! TAKE SOME SHIT!" the one with the bow and arrow says, firing the arrow at the heart of the monster.

"Heh! Why not have a side of light?!" the other one said while slicing the monster in half, and exploding the ever living fuck out of it, blood getting on everything in sight, including Jeremiah.

Jeremiah complains, "Seriously!? Not only did I miss it, I'm now covered in freakin' blood. Oh well." He turns into air real quick and swirls around making a contained high gust wind before remartilizing. He continues walking and sees a wall on a building also covered in blood. "How am I supposed to hang these up now?" He asks right as all the blood that he saw just magically disappears. "Convenient." He gets out some tape from his pocket and starts hanging up a flyer on the wall that says, "Omniverse Pub: Come on down and have a drink or 30." He continues walking, hanging up flyers all over town until he eventually finishes putting up the last one. As he puts all the flyers on walls around town, he noticed a lot of people talking about the fight that just occurred, most saying how the Soular Protection Agency is amazing and what-not. "By the way, what is this Soular Protection Agency? Oh well, not any of my business. I wonder if there's a Pizza Hut nearby?" wonders Jeremiah before going off in search of a Pizza Hut. As he searches for a Pizza Hut, he notices a building with a Huge-Ass-Random Sign Sign saying "Soular Protection Agency! Hiring Now".

Jeremiah looks at his wallet noticing how little there is in there and says, "I don't really like this job anyway." He walks into the building. The inside of it looks like a highly tech-heavy lab, but also has a comforting kind of feel to it….somehow. With two visible people, one covered in blood, the other staring at a Huge-Ass-Random-Computer Computer. While hearing what sounds like a shower happening in the back.

"Ok, so it looks like that we have no more monsters that are located in the city," the one at the computer says, "Well if there is no others, then I guess I have nothing better to do right now then, so I'm going to go change in the back, alright Ra?" the blood-covered one says, who has a greenish-blue trench coat, grayish-blue shirt, dark gray pants and black boots while wearing shades, now hovering above his eyes. (Lyric Hunton, Series: A Megalo Stream, Author: Matthew)

"Mhm. Go right the hell ahead then." Ra says, who's wearing the same greenish-blue trench coat as Lyric, has an eye patch covering his right eye, wearing a golden necklace saying "I'm da Boss!" at the bottom of it, also wearing a gray shirt and a very dark shade of gray pants, while having a nice trim of a beard and sideburns. (Series: Demonic Fellow/Identity Crisis, Author: Matthew), as the other one just goes off to go change.

Jeremiah is starstruck at the place as he mumbles softly, "Just like home." He walks up to Ra and greets, "Hello there. I saw you were hiring and was wondering if you had any positions for a hero or an agent or something?"

"That can be determined, just follow me out back and we shall have a nice little spar to determine if you're good enough for us," he replies.

"No problem," says Jeremiah with vigor and absolute confidence.

Ra takes Jeremiah out back into an arena like area. There's multiple seats for people to sit IF they wanted to but nobody else is there at all. Once in the arena Jeremiah presses a big red button on his gray watch with a strange logo on it causing a green data sphere to appear around him. The sphere downloads his clothes and uploads his bio-suit on him. When it disappears he's in a blue bio-suit. The visor kicks on showing him tactical information. He says, "Where I come from they used to call me the Elemental."

"So you're one of them huh? Well well well, it's nice to finally meet one. And just so we're clear, my name is Ra," he says as another person, having a towel covering most of him while having another towel wrapped around his neck comes out. (Note: Casually wears a green with red stripes hoodie, dark red pants, with red eyes while being buff and 5'9". Chara Dragonic, Series: Demonic Fellow, Author: Matthew)

"What's sup fucker?" they said.

"Hey Chara, mind giving me a sword of yours?"

"You get a knife," Chara says as he gives Ra a red knife, with some black spots.

Jeremiah reaches out his hand and in a brief flash a silver sword with ancient writing appears in his hand. He readies it. "You ready?" he asks with vigor.

"About as ready as Chara over there was the first time I saw them. And he barely put up a fight." Ra said.

"HEY U FUCKER IM RIGHT HERE!" Chara says angrily.

"Wow, rude much," says Jeremiah about Chara's attitude.

"Eh, let him be, he did just fight a huge monster after all, a little light teasing won't hurt no one."

"Whatever. En garde," says Jeremiah as he quickly goes in for a slash at near light speed.

Ra just barely dodges it, kicking Jeremiah in his stomach with enough force to cause him to fall onto his stomach on the ground while feeling a bit winded, but still able to do anything. Jeremiah creates a burst of light energy. While Ra was airborne, Jeremiah quickly stands back up and blasts him with the same energy and nailed him in the gut. Ra just takes it and looks to be barely harmed from it. He starts speed levitating up, goes above Ra, and kicks him down to the ground. Then, Jeremiah disappears as he turns into air. Ra just stops breathing, or so it seems very realistically. Suddenly, the wind starts intensifying and concentrating on Ra cutting him from every angle. Ra just starts looking so pale, not moving, not breathing. It seems to be like Ra was actually killed. The wind stops and Jeremiah reappears. He goes in front of Ra guard up and asks concerned, "Are you ok?" Ra then suddenly grabs Jeremiah's wrist before he could respond at all, and just throws him to the ground on his back. Jeremiah just says, "Interesting." Ra then suddenly pulls Jeremiah in and throws him into the air. Ra quickly floats upwards and slices him into multiple pieces utilizing the borrowed knife. Blue slime suddenly rains down to the ground as Ra comes back down for a soft landing. The pieces of slime start coagulating together and form a giant axe-like pendulum before solidifying and changing its color and properties to that of one and slices Ra vertically. Afterwards, it turns back into slime and changes shape until it turns back into Jeremiah. Before solidifying, it splits into three Jeremiahs and they all solidify and regain their colors. Two of them lung at Ra while one of them begins charging a red sphere in his right hand. A Whip of fire manifests beginning from the hand of the right Jeremiah while the left one's hand catches on fire and he goes in for a punch. The fire whip hits Ra first from a distance knocking him to the side a bit and while stumbling, the other copy rushes him and punches him down to the ground using his blazing hand. The copy's hand goes back to normal before he jumps to the side. The last one jumps above Ra and fires a red beam much more destructive than any of his other attacks thus far creating a huge explosion and crater on impact. He lands and says, "I call that move: Power Blast." Ra just lays there, not moving again, not breathing yet again. Jeremiah's duplicates turn back into blue slime and return to the main body becoming part of him once him. He walks closer to the crater and says to Ra, "Like I'm going to fall for that trick again. Do you surrender?"

He gets no response what-so-ever, but soon sees that part of Ra starts dusting away. Jeremiah observes, "Armor? Or is that a shed skin? Is he reptilian?" He ponders this for a moment and wonders, "Is he even inside there?" Jeremiah's eyes start glowing blue and he uses his Citaloanin sight to see inside the presumed armor, but all he sees is just an empty body, filled with dark gray like dust, fading away with an upside-down heart, cracked from side to side. Its crack seems to be getting worse by the second. His eyes stop glowing and Jeremiah yells to anyone who can hear, "HEY! Is this weird heart-thingy inside him important cause it's about to break!?" Once again, no response comes out. And the heart just breaks, Ra's body completely goes to dust, leaving behind his clothes, and an eye patch. Jeremiah starts panicking and saying, "Oh crap. I disintegrated him. This is bad. This is very bad! Ok, Jeremiah just calm down." He takes a deep breath. His eyes start glowing blue and he looks around the stands, not moving his head, to see if there's any witnesses. While he looks, a yellow beam of pure light encases the dust that was once Ra. The dust and clothes start to float up. The dust forming the shape of Ra yet again and he just pops back into life. Jeremiah is just standing there with a blank expression on his face emphasizing his massive confusion and relief. "What just happened?" His eyes turn back to normal and he looks up at Ra.

"Oh hey, I'm back from the dark void. Good job, Chara." He said as he floats back down onto the ground.

Jeremiah states with the same blank expression, "I have no clue what's going on anymore."

"That's normal for people who are new to SilverKeep. And I can teach you what just happened after I get you kitted out with some new weapons and a uniform," he replies.

Jeremiah presses a button on the wrist of his suit and another green data sphere appears putting back into his regular attire. "So I guess this means I aced the test?" asked Jeremiah hopefully with a nervous smile.

"Yeah, you did. Just, please don't kill me next time will ya?"

"No problem. That doesn't normally happen. If I was still in the Superheroes I might have been fired," says Jeremiah.

Ra then takes Jeremiah to a room filled to the brim with weapons: some knives, some swords, and a whole lot of guns. He then says "Well, here's your selection of what you want to use, so feel free to try out any of it on me if you so need." He then gives Jeremiah a uniform, informing him that this is the Soular Uniform and that when on duty needs to be worn. He replies, "Ok, no problem. Quick question, do they have infinite storage pockets?"

"No, all the high tech stuff were mainly from Chara who is fast asleep at the computer right now," he replies.

"Ok, I'll install them later. I actually learned science and engineering from the prince and princess of Planet Gaxi (Gal-a-za) themselves, before they died that is," states Jeremiah.

"I don't know what you're talking about but ok i guess." Ra replies as he sits down on a chair nearby.

Jeremiah scratches his head and says calmly, "Oh yeah, different dimension. By the way, what's the pay for this job?"

"Pay is $12 an hour, but you only get paid every 2 weeks. Also, just so you know, this job here: is an assassin and /or a hero job," he replies.

"Assassin?" asks Jeremiah nervously.

"Yep, but before anything we will test you for any information you think should be known to us so that you don't get assigned anyone with people you rather keep alive. We do happen to care about who we assign to people and don't want any casualties that you didn't want," he replies.

"So wait, you mean to tell me that my job...is to kill?" asks Jeremiah nervously and cautiously.

"Well yes, but we do also tend to work with the government, police, and what-not and they do know who we kill, what we kill, and when we need to kill them. But we send them info about who we don't want killed before-hand."

The famous line, "You either die a hero or live long enough to become the villain," echoes in his head. What he has wandered into was the exact opposite of his usual mindset, training, and experience. All his previous jobs had a strict, "No-kill unless absolutely necessary" policy and even then he only killed one individual: a supervillain by the name of Darkness. He says, having trouble thinking of the words, "I'll...have to think on it."

"What are you thinking of this job? Do you like what will happen? Or are you thinking that it's more of a villain kind of job?" he asked.

"No offense, but I lived my entire life as a Superhero. I was trained under a strict no-kill policy. Heck, there were at least three manuals of rules to learn in that organization. So yes, this does seem like more of a villain thing to me," plainly states Jeremiah a bit harshly.

"Well, I can assure you, that this is not a villain job. We work to get rid of villains, and there are times where we are strictly told not to kill them, but more often than not we do kill the villains. So i understand if you need a bit of time to think this over, I'm not heartbroken or anything about it. I understand whether you need time to think it over and if you do decide to not take the job," he replies.

"Understood." Jeremiah bows in respect and leaves giving serious thought to his dilemma. He decides to go over to Pizza Hut and order some pizza because he hasn't had lunch yet. Once his pizza got done he began eating it deep in thought about all the hard battles he has fought in his life from Planet Gaxi's invasion to the war against Darkness among countless other battles. He decides instead of moping about it to gather some intel on them. He pays for his pizza and leaves Pizza Hut before going into a dark alley. He turns into blue slime and shapeshifts into a woman with blond hair with green eyes with a slightly curvy figure. "This way they won't recognize me. Now first off, I need to go to the library. I should have the entire day before Alucard comes looking for me."

He/she, now I'm confused, goes over to the library sponsored by Random-Ass-Corporation Inc. and walks over to the librarian who has a very cartoony reaction to whatever gender he/she is with hearts coming out of his eyes and his tongue sticking out. She says, "Hello, I'm looking for information about the Soular Protection Agency. Know where I can find a few books on that?"

He replies "Actually there is an employee from that Agency in the back right now. He could give you some information."

"Cool. Thanks for your assistance."

She walks over to the back of the library and spies the one who originally was covered in blood near Ra when Jeremiah first entered, while wearing a bright blue hoodie now, complete with dark blue pants and still wearing his black shoes, looking at some children's book.

"Let's see…. What book did she say she needed?"

Jeremiah walks up and asks, "What book are you looking for?"

"That I don't know yet." He replies.

"Do you know what it's about?" Jereline asks.

He looks at his phone and summons a decent size wings and flies to the top of the shelf and grabs the book that he needs and comes back down.

"By the way, I heard you work at the Soular Protection Agency? What's it like working there?"

"Honestly, it really is something great. While we don't always get attacks each day, we do tend to normal stuff we would usually do at home when not saving the town from certain damnation. But when we do get attacks, we are there to either get the monster away from the city or flat out kill them. But we will sometimes, not often, get assigned to an assassin mission. But again, that does not happen too often," he answers.

"I see. Who do you usually have to assassinate on these missions?" asked Jereline with a serious tone in her voice.

"Usually we are assigned people who are criminals and have escaped a penalty of some kind," he answers.

"So here, the penalty for escaping from prison is death? Seems kind of harsh," reiterates Jereline to make sure she's got it.

"Well, I mean, we do give them about a few weeks or so before we actually do get assigned to them. We won't always get assigned to them as either we're beaten to it, or the police just gets them before we're even informed on it," he replies.

"Hmm, intriguing. Do you have access to all the classified police records?"

"Not as far as I know. If anything, Ra would know that answer," he replied.

"Hmm, I see. What about threats to the entire planet such as an alien invasion? What do you do about that?" asks Jereline.

"At first, we would get informed by the government themselves, and we're usually sent off to go check it out. And if we need to, we can resort to just killing them right there and then, but more often than not we are under orders to not kill them." He replies.

"I see. How much of this information is not available to the general public?"

"Mainly what we do during the mission. But at times, the general public will be told of certain threats, or other stuff that they need to know," he replies.

"For example, the assassinations? Does the general public know about that?" interrogates Jereline.

"Mainly the major ones are told out to the public. The minor cases aren't as well known however."

"I see. By the way, how advanced is your Agency's technology? Are you capable of space-travel yet?" continues Jereline.

"By normal terms, no, but having the employees having access to magic does in fact make space-travel possible. Though we are still developing a way to make it possible without magic."

"I see. Last question, how big of an offense does it take to be targeted for assassination?"

"Usually breaking the law, being sent to prison, breaking out of it, staying out for a long period of time and committing more crimes is when someone is targeted. But if someone say, was framed, or just simply never done any of it, we do look for solid evidence for it before determining if they're a target or not."

She says, "Ok, by the way if you want to find ways to advance your technology, I highly recommend checking out the Omniverse Pub which is connected throughout all of space and time. There's currently an entrance in the outskirts of SilverKeep if you're interested." After that advertisement she walks away and out of the library. She thinks, *"That was a lot of useful information but just in case I better fact-check it."* Jereline goes around Silverkeep questioning many individuals about the Soular Protection Agency. Many of which do seem to give very similar answers. During the evening she gets a call from Alucard asking where he is. She says, "Don't worry. I'm almost done over here, I'll be over there soon." She hangs up and finally turns to his regular form. He smiles and says, "For the most part, they seem alright. However, I'm not sure how trustworthy they are. Well then, let's go."

He goes back over to the Agency. He then finds Ra, sitting in his chair, looking at the screen. He seems to be talking to someone from the government and not paying attention to anything else. Jeremiah shapeshifts into blue slime and approaches making sure not to alert Ra and eavesdrops on the conversation turning himself into part of the back of the chair.

"Yes sir, all damage that was done to the city today was repaired and already dealt with." Ra says.

"Alright, then, so I assume that this monster was killed then?"

"Yes sir. Killed like you wanted it to be. If anything else comes by we will be sure to take care of it. Unless you need us to go under a No-Kill policy for now."

"That won't be needed for now. Just keep doing what you guys do."

"Alright. Goodbye." Ra hangs up the phone and looks at Jeremiah. "Well now you know what I do in the evenings." Jeremiah turns back into blue slime and back into his normal form, "How did you know?"

"I could sense you the entire time."

"Alright, have you considered just upgrading your containment technology? It'd be a much better solution than killing. I'm sure I got some old Superheroes files on laser bar tech," suggests Jeremiah.

"While I do like the idea, I can't argue that with the government."

"Well then, I just wanted to let you know I thought about your offer and I accept it for now, but I'm not quitting my day job at this time."

"Alright, shall we work on your timeframes for now then? We have some night shift slots open right now."

Suddenly, Jeremiah's phone rings. "Yeah, yeah. I'll be right there I'm just wrapping things up." He hangs up and hands Ra a copy of his schedule for the Pub. "Here's a copy of my schedule for my first job and I got to get back to work so I'll see you later."

"Alright then, take care, I do want you to return at 5:30 pm tomorrow for your schedule alright?"

"Roger, have a good day." He leaves with his final thoughts being, *"I'll just have to change this organization from the inside."*

# Chapter 2: Dimension-Hopping

It's been two weeks since Jeremiah has joined the Soular Protection Agency (SPA) and nothing interesting has happened in those last two weeks. We currently find Jeremiah recounting tales of his hero career to the agents of SPA, all while one is leaving his shift and heading home to just pass out on the floor to sleep for the entire day, leaving two agents left to hear his tales.

"And that is how me and my teammates ended up defeating Darkness and saving the entire multiverse from destruction," concludes Jeremiah.

"That is… actually pretty cool buddy," Lyric says.

"Thanks. However, I'm a bit fuzzy on the details for some strange odd reason. I don't know why. It's as if there are two different sets of memories and I don't know which is which," states Jeremiah.

"Two different sets huh? That's very interesting. Not sure if I can just look into the sets of memories because I'm not sure what the limits are, my abilities aren't really too specific." He says.

"Interesting. I got a magic list of powers that appeared in my pocket from day one," says Jeremiah as he pulls out a mile long list of his powers from his pocket with slightly glowing parchment.

"Ok, wow. We really went to the cartoony reference? I never thought we'd go that low." He replies to the mile-long list.

"Heck, my shape-shifting makes me act like a Loony Toons character sometimes," replies Jeremiah.

"Oh god." He replies.

"I know right? And I'm from a serious storyline," states Jeremiah.

"At least you know what storyline you're from and how developed it is! Mine is just a huge mess of ideas that never made it into the release! I wish all the goddamn time it would just be written already" He states.

"I think that's pretty much every author in existence. Stuff usually doesn't get organized until said author writes it down, and possibly rewrites it several times over. The process varies from author to author," answers Jeremiah.

They can hear a voice from beyond the 4th wall, which says "it's not my fault that i draw more than i write!"

Another voice replies, "It kind of is. Plus you didn't capitalize 'it's'."

"well excuuuuuuuuuuuuse me princess! i prefer to not capitalize anything!" The first voice replies.

Jeremiah yells at the 4th wall, "Hey, we're trying to tell a story here. Plus, capitalization is important for storytelling. You might alienate the readers doing that. This isn't a text message for crying out loud."

"so what? it's just how i type goddamn it! if u want me to cap my stuff, too bad, i refuse to do anything about it!" The first voice replies.

The second voice apologizes, "Sorry about him. This is the problem with collabs. Plus, we're on Google Docs so…"

"ok, can we please just continue the story? assuming i can properly type today jeezus" V1 replies.

There is silence on the other side of the wall.

"Good," says Jeremiah calmly.

"So uh, what shall we do for now?" Lyric asks.

"An excellent question. It's been pretty quiet these past couple of weeks. Could this be the calm before the storm?" theorizes Jeremiah.

"Nah, it's usually quiet here, there's not that much that happens really," Lyric replies.

"I feel like there's usually a new villain to fight at least a couple of weeks or months after the last one. As if I was in some TV show that kept getting renewed for another season," states Jeremiah.

"Not sure what world you live in but uh, it usually takes a while for a new villain to try to kick our asses," he states.

"Oh well. Maybe I'm just a little too used to action. Fighting off alien invasions and intergalactic threats will do that to a person," replies Jeremiah sinking into his beanie bag chair some more.

As he does that, Lyric gets up and goes to another room for a few minutes, but comes back in a hoodie, gray sweatpants, and boots and sits down.

"Well this seems like more of the mood I suppose." He says.

"I suppose," says Jeremiah as he checks his gray, unusually high-tech watch pushing a big red button on it causing it to open up and reveal the time.

"Well, look at the time. I suppose I better head out. See you guys in a bit," says Jeremiah as he gets up and waves goodbye.

Lyric waves back as he gets back to grab his bag to head out as well. They both walk out the door at the same time, but as Jeremiah starts to walk off, a flash of wind suddenly comes out, as he looks behind him he sees a pair of red wings forming on Lyric's back. He mumbles, "Intriguing." Lyric then flies off somewhere.

Jeremiah begins walking and starts thinking to himself, "*Man, it's been two weeks since I got here and I'm no closer to figuring out how their system and protocols work around here. Sure, I've been reading these old manuals in the library, but they're not very helpful. How did I follow all those protocols in the Superheroes to begin with if I'm having this much trouble simply understanding the inner workings of a small-time organization? Oh well. Come to think of it. Maybe I could use some allies in my quest. I'll try giving Elements and Linda a call. Luckily, I was able to utilize some of Ichamar's code for an interdimensional cell phone to develop an app for that in my watch."*

Jeremiah begins fiddling with his watch and opens up the interdimensional phone app. The first screen that appears is a prompt that says, "Insert UVW coordinates here."

*"What the heck are UVW coordinates!? Why do I need coordinates for a simple phone call? Plus, aren't coordinates usually XYZ, not UVW? What kind of crazy dimension is Ichamar from?"* While Jeremiah is over there yelling at his watch internally over the coordinate system, an explosion can be heard from all over the town. Jeremiah looks over towards the direction of the sound. He sees a person, flying in the sky with the use of wings, but they look incredibly black, pure black darkness at that. Jeremiah jumps high into the sky and speed-levitates over to that location. Before he arrives, he presses the button on his watch and a green data sphere envelops him. When it disappears, he's in a blue bio-suit and speeds up. As he arrives, someone else seems to kick the person down to the ground from the sky, but it was so fast that Jeremiah couldn't make out who the other person was.

Jeremiah states looking in the direction of the downed person, "Wow, and to think I can go up to Mach 200 and not see who it was."

He looks towards his opponent further up in the sky. From where he was at, all he could make out was that the person wasn't human, had horns and a tail with a blue tip. Hovering there, charging up a blast with multiple balls of energy, all surrounded by weird skulls that resemble that of an ancient animal wielding horns. One of the horns is broken however, and it seems to only be the head of one and nothing else, just hovering the air around him. Jeremiah suddenly ends up in front of him and punches him, sending him flying into a nearby building.

"I don't know who you are, but I'm not letting you hurt anyone!" declares Jeremiah.

The person who was punched into the building teleports behind Jeremiah and fires a blast of light into the downed opponent. "Killing" them into pieces. Jeremiah hears the shatter and he looks down and sees nothing of his ally. He looks at his opponent and yells, "Where is he? What did you do to him?" The other person just flies off in a hurry, repeating to himself, "Don't stop! Don't stop!" As he tries to follow the darkness opponent through the city. Jeremiah blasts at him with a beam of light energy. It hits him in the back. But it seemed to have no effect." I guess we're doing this the hard way." Jeremiah sped up and slammed into him causing them both to crash into a nearby building of them shattering some windows. They skid across the office floor as Jeremiah pins him down. He charges a red sphere in his free hand.

"If you don't want to face the full front of Power Blast at point-blank range, you better start talking!" demands Jeremiah.

"There's no time left! We need to move again and get ahead of him! He's going to destroy this world if we don't do anything about it! So let me go and let me handle this!" He says right before he kicks Jeremiah off of him causing him to accidentally fire his Power Blast up into the ceiling vaporizing it completely. The guy flies off again yelling out, "I won't die! Not again!"

"Again?" says Jeremiah confused as he gets up.

He jumps and continues pursuit. He ends up right next to the guy and asks hastily, "Who's threatening you and this entire dimension?"

He just doesn't respond but opens up a portal and flies faster into it, going into another dimension in front of a shrine. Jeremiah follows him into the portal before it closes. He notices the orb that is being held in the middle of the shrine as it floats, the other person running towards it and grabbing it close to him.

"Now we have this, but we need to keep it hidden for now."

Jeremiah walks up to him and says, "Look, I have no clue what's going on here or why this particular orb is important, and I'm used to ancient artifacts and legends that detail the destruction of one world or another, but can you just tell me what's going on?" But as they turn around, they see someone else.

"Hello there. Jeremiah. Matt. How are you guys? Or should I say… Guy and Gal?" he greets with a glitched voice.

He looks over at the person he's been chasing for a good majority of this chapter, then he looks back at the owner of the glitched voice, and goes back and forth for a bit before settling on the source of the glitched voice and replying, "So, you've heard of me? I guess my exploits reach out even to here." He says the second sentence while smiling a big wide smile. Matt then summons two blasters around the two, saying "Come at us, only if you want to die, Galgric" Jeremiah looks done with this and runs so fast nobody can see him and grabs the orb out of Matt's hands and is already several feet behind him. "Better talk fast, or this thing is getting shattered."

"IF YOU SHATTER THAT THEN THERE'S NO WORLD!" Matt shouts back.

He looks at the orb stunned in shock and says plainly, "Really? Is that so?" He puts the orb under his armpit and asks, "Wait, which world?" Everyone just stares at him like he just dropped an f-bomb.

"What? We're in a different dimension, I'm from a different dimension from the dimension we were just in. So, it's a valid question," explains Jeremiah.

"If the orb is shattered, then every world, every universe, is destroyed! With the only way of getting them back is through a world reset only I can do!" Matt explains.

He looks at the orb and exclaims while pointing at it, "This don't look like the Space Core! And I met it. Course, I don't know it nearly as well as the Time Core."

The glitched out voice calls out, "Why not give me the orb then? It will be much more suited for me then that idiot."

"No offense lady, dude? I don't know. But if it's as important as you say it is, my first thought is to **not** hand it over to random strangers I just met and instead get out of here before someone (His left arm glows pink and a pink portal appears behind him.) has the chance to yell 'Objection'." He runs into the pink portal which instantly closes.

"Well that happened?" Matt says.

Jeremiah ends up in front of a school. He goes inside the schoolyard and goes to a corner of the building with faded out letters. He inputs a sequence of them revealing an entrance at a different point in the school. He goes over to the entrance and types in a password in the keypad next to it before scanning his finger. The small hatch opens, and he goes in it sliding down to a secret base. The hatch closes automatically and hides itself once more. He arrives down in his secret base formerly known as Sector 17. His allies, a young woman with jet black hair and pink eyes wearing green attire and a young man with a blue leather jacket, sunglasses, brown hair and looks like a biker were just doing who knows what. They instantly see Jeremiah and the biker greets, "Yo, I haven't seen you in a couple of weeks? How's the janitorial job coming along?"

"I hate it so much, but I was able to snag a second job with something closer to hero work," answers Jeremiah.

"Nice," replies the blue biker giving him a thumbs up.

The young woman gets up and asks pointing to the orb Jeremiah was holding, "What's with the sphere?"

"Well Linda, that's the weird thing. Apparently, this is some sort of...other Space Core. I don't know how there's two of them, but apparently there's people trying to snag it claiming its destruction will cause the end of the multiverse so that's a thing," explains Jeremiah to the best of his ability yet still confused on the matter.

"Isn't this Darkness all over again?" asks the biker.

"No, this seems more like Master Dark's plan, which you weren't there for either of those events. Either way, we need to protect this sphere at all cost," says Jeremiah in response to the biker.

"So another ancient legend that predicts the end of the world. How cliche," states Linda dryly.

"Yeah, I know. Not much I can do about it. By the way, I need your help with something," states Jeremiah.

"What is it?" asks Linda.

"Probably to protect that sphere," chimes in the blue biker.

"Well, yes that. And that organization I'm working with apparently thinks it's ok to kill people so I'm trying to change it from within," answers Jeremiah.

Elements exclaims, "Hold on a minute! Use your words and explain to us in more detail what the frick you've been doing these past couple of weeks."

Jeremiah explains everything that has been going in the Soular Protection Agency especially around its killing policy while both the biker and Linda listen intently.

"Yeah, it's a lost cause," says the biker.

"Lost cause!? What do you mean by lost cause?" shouts Jeremiah.

"It's a government sanctioned organization and they're not going to listen to some peon about how 'wrong' or 'immoral' their killing philosophy is. Take it from a former peon disguised as a general," argues the biker.

"I honestly have to agree with Elements on this one. You're really too naive for your own good. Besides, sometimes killing people is necessary. Remember when we faced Darkness, you had to kill him for the sake of the multiverse," comments the young woman.

"That was different Linda," states Jeremiah aggressively before Linda counters, "How would you know!? You've only been there for a couple of weeks. You don't know the dangers they face on a day-to-day basis."

Jeremiah looks down at the floor questioning himself. Linda's point hit deep. He has no clue what he's doing, and he doesn't know whether the change would be for the better or not. As he sinks deeper into thought Linda says, "Listen, don't lose your sense of hope. Besides, just because we don't agree with you doesn't mean we won't help you. Your heart's in the right place but your head isn't. We'll be glad to help you just so long as you don't get in over your head. Plus, I would rather not have you attacked for that Space Core."

Elements chimes in, "I'm down. It's getting boring just staying here and waiting for something. I haven't fought a good villain since that Ancient Egyptian of Time. In hindsight, that is a terrible name for him."

As Elements readjusts his sunglasses, Jeremiah's face lights up and he says, "Thanks, but are you two really cool with that since you just disagreed with me?"

"Yes, we're just going to be there so you don't do something stupid," argues Linda.

Elements yells, "You will if we leave you to your own devices."

Jeremiah looks at him plainly and says, "You have zero faith in me, what-so-ever."

"Well duh. You're great in a fight but you're too idealistic, and stubborn," answers Elements.

"So what do we do with Space Core 2.0 over here?" asks Jeremiah.

"I say we gather up all the Gaxi (Gal-a-za) tech we can get our hands on and take it to this new dimension. If he got to that one dimension, he can probably get to this one too. It's only a matter of time before he shows up."

"Alright, Elements, Linda. You two will gather up all the Gaxi tech we currently have at Sector 17. I'll grab the Stormbreaker and fly over to Planet Gaxi and get some more equipment for analyzing the Space Core 2.0. Why do I have this nagging feeling the original Space Core doesn't like my naming scheme?" orders Jeremiah.

"What about that sphere anyway?" asks Linda pointing at the dubbed "Space Core 2.0".

"I'll take it with me as a precaution. Plus, it will be easier for the Gaxi technicians if they know what I need the equipment for. Man, I miss Tech Boy and Tech Girl. They would be a huge help right about now."

"Yeah, but they're dead. And last time I checked, you can't revive the dead," replies Elements.

"No, I can't. Now everyone. Get to work!"

Meanwhile

In an alternate dimension

"....WHERE THE FU-"

# Chapter 3: Shenanigans

Jeremiah is currently on his way to Planet Gaxi when suddenly, a random meteorite appears out of the middle of nowhere and **somehow** collides with the Stormbreaker knocking Jeremiah off course sounding various alarms in his ship.

"Ah, crap. Where did that even come from? It didn't appear on radar whatsoever."

Jeremiah shoots past Planet Gaxi and is on course to Planet Thermal, Gaxi's neighboring planet.

"Crap. I can't regain control of the ship and I'm gonna crash. I better brace for impact."

Jeremiah enters Thermal's atmosphere and his ship begins to heat up and starts to break apart due to damage from the impact. He braces himself for a crash landing when a random vortex appears in the exact spot he's going to crash in and he falls in it right before it disappears. He now finds himself in a dark void.

"Am I back in space? I don't see any stars or interstellar matter for that matter."

He checks the radar, but nothing is there.

"Odd."

He presses a button on his watch and a green data sphere envelops him converting him into data and downloading his clothes before uploading his old Superhero uniform onto him. Afterwards, it remartilizes him and the data sphere recedes back into his watch. Jeremiah presses a button on the side of his helmet and a blue panel comes out of the sides and covers his mouth and it looks like there's a weird glowing orange splotch on it. He opens the cockpit and levitates out. As he levitates out of the ship, his colors grow dark, to the point that he looks like he's just like outlines but has a blue glow at his chest.

Jeremiah thinks, *"What the frick? This is weird. At least I don't have to worry about oxygen while my suit is on."*

He continues to levitate upwards and he suddenly sees a bright yellow glow coming from his right, it seems to be getting stronger and brighter. Jeremiah continues levitating towards the light. As he gets closer to the light, a figure seems to materialize out of dust surrounding Jeremiah, like the very concept of the location is filled with nothing but dust. Suddenly the figure starts to harden and it's colors go just as dark as Jeremiah's did, but a red glow appears at the chest, with what seems to be a green sweater with gray stripes on it.

Chara appears and asks, "HEY!? Are you fucker in here?"

Jeremiah responds, "Are you sure you said that sentence right?"

Chara responds, "Are you a freakin grammar nazi?"

Jeremiah answers, "No, it just doesn't sound right to me. So, where are we?"

Chara then jumps into the void and, using fire magic formed in his hands, he speedily flies towards Jeremiah and he braces for impact.

Chara says as he stops near him, "Welcome to the death void. This is the place where you go when you die. I've been here a fuck ton of times and I know how to enter and exit out of this awful place…. Only when I'm a alive fucker tho. Dead not so much."

"Do you normally enter here via random vortex as you're crash-landing on a planet?" asks Jeremiah not thinking about how ludicrous that sounds.

"Yes.. totally happens to me every time I want to enter this- OF FUCKING COURSE NOT! I USE MAGIC U DUMBASS" Chara replies.

"Really. That's how I got in here. My ship is over there if you don't believe me," says Jeremiah pointing to his ship when he mentioned it.

"Yeah I saw. Kinda hard not to stare at your dumbass piloting as you go into the vortex. Like seriously, how do you make something as stupid as a freakin metor appear out of thin fucking nowhere and crash land in the death void!?" He responds.

Jeremiah makes an "I don't know" gesture in response to that.

"Great. That's helpful, totally helpful." Chara responds before grabbing Jeremiah's literal ass and drags him back out of the void. He also pulls out a cigarette out of his pocket and puts it in his mouth, lighting it using fire magic from his hands.

"I never said you could grab my butt. Why didn't you just take my arm? Why my butt specifically?"

"Because I rather drag your dumb ass out of here instead of your dumb arm….. dumbass."

Jeremiah shapeshifted his butt into spikes and pierces Chara's hand. He did not take kindly to that insult.

In response, Chara says sarcastically, "Oh nooo, you shapeshifted your ass into spikes, OHH IT HURTS! OWW! It totally hurts. Oh please don't hurt me more senpai!" And grips harder to not lose Jeremiah, who is looking at him in sheer disappointment with a blank expression, and they go out of the void and land on Planet Gaxi, with Jeremiah coming out of the portal and landing on his ass. Chara takes his hand out of his spikes, which Jeremiah retracts afterwards, and his left eye goes green and his hand heals completely.

"My disappointment is immeasurable right now. By the way, how long have you've been watching me?" says Jeremiah.

"I actually needed Ra to tell me the exact cords that you were at before I could actually go in there and get your ass. I just knew you were in there because of my senses." Chara responded.

Jeremiah gets back up and staring at Chara right in the face says, "Yeah, but you also mentioned the meteor that hit the ship, which I never told you about. So how could you have known that?"

"Because I'm Chara, I can do that sorta thing." He replies.

"Not buying it. I need a more logical explanation," states Jeremiah.

"WE ARE LITERALLY IN A FAKE CHAPTER WE CAN DO ANYTHING WE WANT! And I felt like making a reference bitch." Chara says.

Jeremiah grabs Chara by the shirt, says, "In that case," and then opens a portal to Planet Thermal's cold side and throws Chara in there before closing it and finishing, "Enjoy Planet Thermal! Say hi to the Thermalglobs!"

Jeremiah feels something slap him on the back of his head and then feels something burning his hair. "Are you really sure you can get rid of me that easily? I literally survived -2°C weather." Chara says, while being directly behind Jeremiah.

"I think the cold side of Planet Thermal gets colder than that, but I never went to confirm that. Now would you kindly stop trying to burn my hair before I have to whoop your butt," warns Jeremiah calmly.

"Oh please, like I'm scared of you. I've had to face Satan himself. And he's not even that strong." Chara states.

"Darkness. Multiversal threat. Weren't you there for the story?" asks Jeremiah with a smug expression turning his head towards Chara.

"Wasn't that in Chapter 2 or something? Or was that in Chapter 1?" Chara asks before checking the script of the last two chapters and says, "Yeah, I was never involved in anything, or so I see anyway that it doesn't mention me in the chapters. Besides, you act like I've never faced something like that before."

A burst of light energy erupts from Jeremiah in a sphere that knocks Chara away from him and Jeremiah turns around and says, "You didn't have an appearance in Chapter 2, **but** you had a cameo in Chapter 1 when you handed Ra the knife."

"**SOOO?** I don't give a flying fuck about whether or not I actually saw the events take place. If anything, Matt's the one-" He gets cut off as someone else appears.

"Ah, sir, her name is Ioy now." The person says.

"...Was it really that long ago? Jeezus christ, okay take two people!" He says before going back to what he was saying. "**SOOO?** I don't give a flying fuck about whether or not I actually saw the events take place. If anything, Ioy's the one whose the main character, I'm just a backup main character in the lores...except my own but even then, it's like… a 123 out of 10 on a depression scale." Chara states.

"I don't know what depression has to do with continuity, but it doesn't matter. If Darkness isn't enough, I have also beaten numerous gods, primarily of destruction. Now, why don't we cease this pointless arguing before…"

And then their conversation was suddenly interrupted when the military attacked creating a thick cloud of smoke.

"Okay who invited the fire nation?!" Chara asked

Incredibly futuristic tanks roll up and aim their gigantic frickin laser cannons at them and they begin to charge up. As they charge, Chara summons a knife, but this knife has a gray blade and Chara raises it high in the air. The blade changes colors into that of a deep blood red color and he slices the ground with it creating earthquake level destruction on the planet.

"Take that motherfuckers!!" Chara says.

Jeremiah speed levitates out of the smoke and smashes another one with only his elbow. More tanks surround them. He cracks his knuckles and says, "Is that all you got? I figured you people would know it takes more than that-" He gets interrupted as a Random-Ass-Cinder-Block cinder block launches at his head, sending him flying in the air…

"Cinder blocks. My age-old enemy. Ok, not really, but I felt like saying it," says Jeremiah before an alarm sounds. Suddenly, the palace opens up into four sections as a giant Random-Ass-Mech Mech comes out of the palace. Jeremiah stands up and says cockily, "Now that's more like it."

"Did…. we really need the giant robot?" Chara asked, before leaping at the mech and completely destroying it with one kick. Launching back at the mech after landing on the side of the palace and blasts it with darkness, destroying it completely. "It's not even a challenge."

"You think they would at least invest in an auto-regenerating robot," says Jeremiah triggering the red flag that dictates the robot can now regenerate.

"GOD DAMN IT JEREMIAH! WHY WOULD YOU SAY ANYTHING?! NOW YOU TRIGGER ANIME-STYLED-FIGHT-TRIGGERS TO HAVE IT AUTO-GENERATE ITSELF!" Chara yells at Jeremiah.

"I wanted an epic giant robot fight! And it's auto-regenerate, not auto-generate!" yells back Jeremiah as the robot pieces itself back together before slamming Chara back into the ground creating a crater in the process, leaving Chara in the most famous pose to ever exist, only for Chara to get right the hell back up and say, "Well there's your Dragonball Z reference people, back to your regularly scheduled 19-episode-long-anime-fights." He launches at the robot and completely surrounds it with darkness and crushes it into a tiny cube of robot.

"Was this what Cubix was all about?" asks Jeremiah as he slices up the rest of the tanks causing them all to explode. Cannonballs are fired at them. Jeremiah dodges them while saying, "For a planet that prides itself on-" He gets interrupted again, by Chara saying "NO! DON'T YOU FUCKING DARE TRIGGER ANOTHER ANIME-STYLE-PHRASE!" He says before he takes one tiny step to the right, dodging a cannonball.

Jeremiah lands right next to him and says, "I wasn't going to trigger any flags but since you said something." He grabs Chara, spins around, and tosses him towards the palace. Then he says, "That's for taking my screentime!"

Chara is now flying towards the open palace as he just causally flies in a pose that says "im so done with this bitch" and says to the camera, "So you finally got around to writing more of this stupid chapter? I was wondering if i was gonna be stuck in the middle of fucking air forever."

A voice says, "Well excuse me for being a busy college student. Scratch that, I'm now a graduate. So I was doing good to find any time for fun."

Chara crashes into the palace, making ANOTHER giant hole in the ground to land an epic anime–that-is-famous-enough-already pose at the bottom of it and says "Well there's another one, how many of these Dragonball Z references is there gonna be?!"

A voice says "not enough."

"Well fuck you then." Chara replies.

Next to Chara is a tall, thin scientist with black hair and looking rather regal who asks surprised, "What just happened?"

Jeremiah lands in the underground lab and greets, "Galaxian. You think you can call off the military while you still have some dignity left? Oh wait…"

"Is that how you ask a king in command of a mighty army to back off?" angrily yells Galaxian.

"Probably not, but I pretty much totaled all the forces you sent so far, so…"

While the two were going back and forth Chara found a neat little button that pretty much broke all the robots that were not only outside the lab, BUT also inside the lab! Many machines exploded everywhere, but the most powerful one just so happens to be under

Jeremiah and Galaxian. They explode and they both hit the wall at such a force…… nothing happens.

+0 Damage.

"Friend of yours?" passive-aggressively asks Galaxian.

"If he were, you think he wouldn't be trying to blow me up?"

"Then, is he an ally? Enemy?"

"Coworker."

"Ahh. You want to team up to kill him and we forget this whole charade?"

"You know that I have a strict 'no killing' policy."

A voice says, "Plus this chapter was promoted to an alternate timeline, so…"

Another voice starts chanting "Dew it! DEW IT!"

Jeremiah exclaims, "Are you serious!?"

"Yes."

"oh i crave alllllllllllllllllllllll the violence! dew it before someone diiiiiiiiies"

Galaxian says, "In that case, since you so rudely barged on my planet, destroyed my entire military, I can now legally declare war on you and kill you!"

The floor opens up as a giant mech suit rises out of the ground with Galaxian in the pilot's seat. He grabs Jeremiah with a mechanical claw and slams him in the ground. The other arm's claw recedes into itself and fires a big laser shot at Chara hitting him directly. Whom of which just stands there and takes it, as the smoke clears it shows that he hasn't even moved a muscle and just jumps at the mech, destroying it with a single punch.

"ONE PUNCCCCH!" he says.

"There's a reason why Saitama always arrives late. Because if he showed up right at the beginning, the action scenes would be too short," explains Jeremiah disappointment visible in his face.

Galaxian looks at them, covered in soot from the resulting explosion, with a "oh crap" expression and runs to the escape pods. The door slams shut and he launches into orbit and out of it.

"I hope that doesn't come back to bite us in the rear."

"GOD DAMN IT JEREMIAH YOU MADE IT SO IT WILL LATER ON IN THIS STUPID THING! FUCK YOU FOR THE POINTING IT OUT IN THE FIRST PLACE!" He yells.

"Should I state what else I'm thinking because that will probably end this chapter on a cliffhanger?" asks Jeremiah genuinely.

Chara replies "sure you fucking idiot" as the screen fades out, and JoJo music plays, the "To Be Continued" arrow comes in!


Th-th-th-th-t-t-thats all folks!

Tune in next time for another episode of TOTAL! DRAMA! NOT CANON!


For the real Chapter 3, go to one of these links: (cue in Matt silently giggling to himself)

https://www.wattpad.com/1166977815-a-former-superhero-by-pokemiah-and-futureverse

https://www.fictionpress.com/s/3347358/3/A-Former-Superhero-by-Pokemiah-and-FutureVerse

https://vocal.media/fiction/a-former-superhero-chapter-3-planet-gaxi-supply-run

# You're Still Here?

9 798411 820867